Praise for V

"A long-overdue prescription for engaging the heart. A must-read for all couples who want to enrich their relationship."

David Irvine, author of *Simple Living in a Complex World*

"Such an easy read; it goes down as easy as orange juice and it's great for your relationship!"

Dr. Sue Johnson, director of the Ottawa Couple and Family Institute, and author of *The Practice of Emotionally Focused Marital Therapy: Creating Connection*

"The healing power of a loving relationship has never been so clearly stated."

Bob Urichuck, author of *Online for Life: The 12 Disciplines for Living Your Dreams*

"A super resource for couples. Luke touches on many excellent topics that stimulate meaningful discussion. We use it extensively throughout our marriage preparation/communication course."

Deanne and John Donohue, marriage preparation course conductors

"There is a ton of conflicting information out there about relationships. Luke makes sense of it all for us!"

Wayne McKinnon, the Information Technology Coach™, and author of *Wayne McKinnon's Complete Guide to E-Mail*

"*Vitamin C for Couples* is excellent! This book is a gift to couples and anyone looking to improve their relationships and enjoy a healthier and happier life. Luke has included many important and sensitive topics that people often overlook in their attempts to develop an enriching relationship with their partner. In the hurry-up pace of today's society, Vitamin C is just what the doctor ordered!"

Jim P. Moore, author of *The Mentor: a tale of discovery*

Vitamin C for Couples

Seven "C"s for a Healthy Relationship

Luke De Sadeleer

Books that inspire, help and heal

Published by Creative Bound Inc.
P.O. Box 424, Carp, Ontario
Canada K0A 1L0
(613) 831-3641
www.creativebound.com

ISBN 0-921165-68-4
Printed and bound in Canada

Book design by Wendelina O'Keefe
Author photograph by Van's Studio Limited

Printing number 10 9 8 7 6 5 4 3 2 1

Canadian Cataloguing in Publication Data

De Sadeleer, Luke
Vitamin C for couples : seven "C"s for a healthy relationship

Includes bibliographical references.
ISBN 0-921165-68-4

1. Love. 2. Intimacy (Psychology) 3. Interpersonal Relations. I. Title.

HQ801.D48 2000 158.2 C00-900676-1

This Book Is Dedicated

To my best friend, lover, confidante and loving partner, Susan. For over 20 years you have stood by me, supported and challenged me. You have taught me more about love and relationships than all the courses I have taken and books I have read.

Acknowledgments

Hundreds of people have influenced the creation of this book. I deeply appreciate all you have given me. My sincere thanks to:

The couples and individual clients who allowed me to be part of their struggle. Your willingness to share of yourselves and your lives has taught me so much over the years. A special thank you to those who allowed me to tell their stories in this book.

The many educators, authors and counselors who continue to stretch my learning. You have provided me with a great toolkit.

Dr. Michel Dandeneau who is always ready to listen, provide support and share his insights. You are a true mentor.

Dr. Susan M. Johnson who provided a big piece of the puzzle. Thank you for teaching your incredible work and developing what is rapidly becoming the best approach to working with couples.

Susie Moncur and inscape publishing, formerly Carlson Learning Company, for allowing me to illustrate portions of the *Personal Profile System®*.

Bob Urichuck who has helped me to develop my career as a professional speaker. I will always be grateful for your suggestions and motivation.

James Zito who contributed valuable research and information.

The book production team: Gail Baird and Barb Clarke, designer Wendy O'Keefe and editor Deanne Donohue. You brought it all together and helped to create a book that would appeal to a universal audience.

Our sons, daughter-in-law and granddaughters: Michael, Dean,

June, Sarah, Emily and Mackenzie, for teaching me the real meaning of family and connection.

Finally, and most important, my loving partner, Susan, who helped me to put theory into practice and allowed me to share so many of our learning experiences with you, the reader, so that you may benefit from our mistakes and triumphs.

Contents

Introduction

How *Vitamin C for Couples* Will Help You

Do you want to be happier, healthier and live a longer life? I'm sure you answered "yes" to this question. However, you may be surprised to know that one of the best ways to achieve all three is to have a secure and loving relationship.

You are most likely aware of the benefits of exercising, eating the right foods and taking your vitamins. You know that doing these things will improve your health and extend your lifespan. However, you may not know that it has been proven that close, loving relationships have just as much, if not more, to do with our health and longevity. Human beings need relationships not only for our well-being, but also for our survival.

You will learn that anything you do to increase the love, security, closeness and connection in your intimate relationship will not only keep you healthier, it will improve the quality and duration of your life. Love is the elixir of youth. I guess the Beatles were pretty close to the truth when they sang, "Love is all you need."

When it comes to being happier, many people assume that to achieve this goal they only need to have a higher standard of living. They confuse standard of living with quality of life. The fact is that

a high standard of living has very little to do with our level of happiness. You need only look at the number of people who have everything they need in the way of worldly possessions, and yet are suffering from depression, or are addicted to drugs or alcohol.

Over the years I have counseled many hard-working and successful people. These men and women would reveal to me that even though they excelled in their chosen profession, they found life to be meaningless and empty. They came seeking relief from the loneliness. These diligent people had assumed that happiness would be theirs as soon as they made it to the top. But instead, they found misery, and were suffering from a variety of emotional and physical ailments, including stress, anxiety, ulcers and insomnia. When asked what, if anything, they had done to improve their health and well-being, most of these men and women were proud to express their devotion to exercise and good nutrition. Their intimate relationships, however, were starving for attention and nurturing.

Vitamin C for Couples will help illustrate that true happiness and health do not come from fame and fortune, nor solely investing in your physical well-being. The real-life stories and research presented here will show that your very lives depend greatly on your fulfilling and close relationships.

The best medicine does not always come from a pill or a bottle. Most often, it comes from our relationships with the important people in our lives and especially the intimate relationship with our loving partner. Therefore, I strongly suggest that you share this book with your partner. It is not meant to be read alone. Together you will benefit much more than if only one of you applied the principles presented on these pages.

Remember, you are a couple. You have formed a partnership. Great partners work together to achieve a common goal. My hope is that your goal is to make a good relationship even better. Meeting this goal will contribute to a happy, healthy and long life.

Why This Book?

It is hard to describe how rewarding an experience it is for me when I can help a couple take control of their lives and recover the passion in their relationship. I will admit I just love working with couples. It is my true passion.

Over the past twenty years, while practicing as a psychotherapist, I have seen many couples. However, I was aware that many more couples were resistant to seeking help. Often, one or both partners were reluctant to go to a psychotherapist or a counselor because they assumed that seeking help from "one of these people" meant there was something wrong with them. Recently there has been a growing trend for executives to seek out a coach to help them be more effective in managing their relationships at work. In fact, many see it as a status symbol to have a personal and confidential coach. Just like Olympic and professional athletes know the value of a personal trainer to improving performance, I recognized that couples would benefit from a coach as well. So I decided to call myself a couple's coach. Couples can reach me through e-mail: **luke@thecouplescoach.com** or visit my Web site: **www.thecouplescoach.com**

I also began to apply a preventative approach to working with couples. Just like a coach, I now work with couples to help them improve their relationships and make them stronger. I began this preventative approach because too often couples will wait until their problems have reached such a critical level that many say they are ready to split up. I had frequently wished they would come sooner, before things got desperate and they were experiencing an unhealthy relationship. I knew that if they had started working on their relationship sooner, they would not have experienced such a high level of pain and struggle.

I also knew that many of these same individuals, if they were experiencing a physical illness, would not wait until the situation

became critical before they would go to a doctor. In fact, many had begun a practice of eating and living more healthily, and they believed in the value of taking Vitamin C for maintaining a healthy immune system. They had learned that physical problems could often be prevented if they kept their bodies in better shape.

My preventative approach with relationships is having a growing appeal. Just as many people have learned to prevent problems with their physical well-being, they now apply the same principles to the well-being of their relationship. My suggestion that couples not wait until there is a major problem with their relationship before they do something about it, is being widely accepted.

This acceptance is leading to an increased number of couples who are improving certain skills and behaviors, such as caring, communication, creativity and dealing with conflict. They have formed better and healthier relationships. Applying these same skills in our own relationship, Susan and I have experienced similar results.

I have developed this concept further and have settled on seven important "C"s. The prescription for a healthier relationship is now: **Caring, Change, Communication, Connection, Conflict, Creativity and Commitment.** I call this prescription: *Vitamin C for Couples: Seven "C"s for a Healthy Relationship.*

How to Take *Vitamin C for Couples*

This book has been written using the **KISS** (**K**eep **I**t **S**hort and **S**imple) principle. It is divided into seven chapters, with each of these covering one of the "C"s. The information presented derives from my own experience in working with couples, my personal relationship with my loving partner, case studies and research.

You will discover that I believe very strongly in the value of a loving relationship, and that we need to do whatever is necessary to make it stronger and healthier. I realize you may not agree with everything I suggest or believe. And that's OK. Please feel free to choose those areas that mean the most to you. Use what works for you.

To get the most from this book, I recommend that you review each chapter with your loving partner. Since each chapter builds on a previous one, you may find it more beneficial to read and review them in order. You may also find that certain chapters relate more to you than others.

You will find at the end of each chapter some self-awareness exercises and suggestions. Also at the end of this book is a self-contract. This self-contract is meant to be completed by both you and your partner, specifying the promises you have made to each other. As you complete each chapter, transfer your promise to your self-contract.

Working on relationship issues requires working as a couple, an equal partnership. Working together you will discover the power of a loving partnership. I am firmly convinced that if you practice the seven "C"s described in this book, and follow through on the promises you make, it will help you to make a good relationship even better.

My wish for you is that you will create a healthy relationship that will withstand any challenge, and that together with your loving partner you will experience powerful bonding events that will lead to greater intimacy and joy.

Caring

A loving relationship is one that promotes individual growth and the capacity to care.

The Promise

"I will care for you for the rest of my life!"

What a beautiful promise! What a loving thing to do! Actually, caring implies loving. It is the giving and sharing that is the essence of caring. When we say we care for our partner, we are really saying that we are actively concerned for their life and growth. We are also showing a genuine concern for the health of our relationship. After all, a relationship is like a living thing that needs to be fed and nurtured if it is to grow and develop.

When we nurture and care for each other, we are ensuring that our relationship will remain healthy and strong—something that is necessary for our own physical well-being. It is a fact that human beings need relationships just like they need to eat and drink. Caring for your partner and being cared for is one of the best things you can do

for your health. Research has proven that a relationship affects our body and influences our biological processes. We also know that people who have strong and loving relationships enjoy better health.

The Caring Touch

There are many studies that have proven the need for loving relationships and even physical contact. John Bowlby, for example, studied the effects of early separation on the children evacuated from London during the Second World War. Rene Spitz, on the other hand, looked into the institutions that cared for sick or abandoned children, like pediatric wards and orphanages. Both of them confirmed that if children were not held enough, or played with during their early years, they would never reach their full potential. These babies also suffered from physical deformation, and many died. It did not matter that they were fed and clothed properly, and that their physical needs were met. Lack of proper loving care resulted in sickly babies who were more susceptible to infection and disease. A sterile environment and scientifically applied methods of nurturing and feeding proved to be a bad replacement for good old-fashioned human contact and caring.

This lack of caring is not only detrimental for the survival of small helpless children but affects adults as well. In his book *Feelings*, Willard Gaylin describes what happened when the first "intensive care units" were designed and put into operation. These special units were provided for the sickest patients. They were free of human contamination, and provided constant mechanical attention. Television monitors, electrodes and computers kept a constant vigilance on these critically ill patients. Unfortunately, to the designers' great surprise, the death rate in these modern facilities went up instead of down. Isolation and mechanization, it seems, are no substitute for human care. As stated so well by Dr. Gaylin: "At this time particularly, we need care…anxious concern. And no machine feels that."

So you see, no amount of scientific medicine can replace a caring practitioner. The laying on of hands is still the best medicine. Leo Buscaglia was right when he encouraged all loving partners to hug each other on a regular basis. He also believed that it was the healthiest and most caring act you could do for your relationship.

Take the case of Pat and Cindy. Pat had grown up in a home where hugs and physical signs of affection were not often given. He could not recall a moment where his mother or father had held him in a warm and loving embrace. He described that the periods of physical contact were usually brief and seemed artificial. His wife, Cindy, described Pat as a warm and affectionate husband. However, she was concerned about how Pat responded whenever she would give him a hug or a warm embrace. She said, "He seems to stiffen up, and wants to pull away from me." Pat, like many people who are rarely hugged during their early years, was uncomfortable with receiving hugs. He had not realized how much he tended to shrink away from his partner's attempts to show him affection.

Eventually Pat learned to feel the comfort of a loving embrace. It took the repeated efforts of Cindy holding him in her arms, while he consciously allowed himself to feel his discomfort, before he could relax. Pat became aware of how much he had missed for most of his life. Gradually he enjoyed, and even looked forward to, the hugs that Cindy so willingly gave.

By now I am sure you understand why I feel so strongly about creating a loving and caring environment, where both partners are concerned for the well-being of the other. You may also understand why I frequently state during my workshops and speeches that, "sex is not just for procreation and recreation. It is one of the best activities for our very survival. It helps us to stay healthy and live longer." I also encourage all participants to give a daily loving hug, a love pat, a stroke or a back-scratching to their partners.

I suggest that you include some acts of caring touching as part of

your caring behaviors to be transferred to your self-contract at the end of this book.

Caring Reduces Stress

Stress is a killer. It's as simple as that. Therefore, anything you can do to reduce the negative stress in your life and to increase your resistance to stress will definitely increase your health and your lifespan. In case you are not familiar with how our body responds to stress, here are just a few of the symptoms you may be experiencing:

1. As blood is directed to your muscles and brain, your digestion slows. You're probably experiencing "butterflies" in your stomach.
2. Your breathing gets faster. You may find it hard to catch your breath.
3. Your heart rate goes up, and so does your blood pressure.
4. You find yourself waking up at 4:00 a.m., unable to go back to sleep.
5. You feel irritable and get angry with those who are nearest and dearest.
6. You start to feel tense. Muscles feel tight. You may experience lower back problems.
7. Your immune system is under attack. You are more susceptible to colds and flu.

Now in case you are wondering why this is an important topic for couples to understand, the following studies may convince you. People who are suffering from a stress-related problem make 75 percent of all visits to a doctor. A recent study published by the Canadian Heart and Stroke Foundation revealed that 43 percent of Canadians suffered from stress. That means that for every two people who are reading this book, one of you is likely suffering from

stress. The numbers are staggering. The cause is also disturbing. This study listed the main causes as being related to home, family and work.

A US study conducted over 15 years ago revealed similar frightening results. In the book *Stress Management,* Dr. Edward Charlesworth and Dr. Ronald Nathan list the following results:

1. 30 million Americans have some form of major heart or blood vessel disease.
2. 1 million Americans have a heart attack every year.
3. 25 million Americans have high blood pressure.
4. 8 million Americans have ulcers.
5. 12 million Americans are alcoholics.
6. 5 *billion* doses of tranquilizers are prescribed each year.

You can imagine what the current numbers are. No wonder some people say that we are living in the "Age of Anxiety."

By now you may be asking, "What can I do about it?" Well, my answer is that the best way to cope with and reduce stress in your life, is to have a loving relationship. Basically it involves caring.

One of my mentors explained this caring concept to me many years ago when we were conducting stress seminars. Dr. Michel Dandeneau revealed to me that people would reduce their level of stress and increase their health if they took care of at least one of the 3 "P"s. He clarified that each of these "P"s represents a living thing—Plants, Pets and People. For our purpose here, I'd like you to make one of these "P"s, your loving Partner. Amazing, isn't it, that caring for your partner will reduce your stress? Believe me, it works.

Another thing to know about stress, is that it is actually easy to explain its cause. Stress is caused by control, or at least the lack of it. If you have control over a situation your stress will go down. On the other hand, if you lose control, or lack control, your stress will go up. The example I usually give, goes as follows: Stress is being told you had the winning ticket to the lottery, when you can't find the ticket.

Whether or not you find this example humorous, the fact remains that many people start their day wishing for a winning ticket. It is much more likely, however, that life will confront us with more challenges—challenges that are best faced with a caring partner. You and your partner will feel more in control of life's challenges if you work together as a team. Having similar goals and supporting each other will definitely reduce your stress.

I am not denying that exercise and eating the right foods will also contribute to good stress management. However, I firmly believe that a stable and loving relationship is even better. We need security and predictability. We need to belong. We want to avoid disagreements and conflict. We need to be accepted and respected. We need an environment where we can relax and replenish our energy. All of these needs, if they are not met, will increase the stress in our lives.

We used to be able to count on the consistency and predictability of our families. In times of crisis they were there to help. Unfortunately, in today's society, extended families are less often the norm. Our workplaces are also less predictable and supportive. Studies show that the new work environment greatly contributes to the stress in our lives. In the era of downsizing, restructuring and cutbacks, insecurity and unpredictability are part of our culture. Is it any wonder that often the only place in which we can find safety and security is in our intimate relationship?

So remember, nurture your relationship. Care for your partner. The very act of caring for a living being will contribute to *your* well-being.

Regardless of the stress the world throws at you, and believe me stress is unavoidable, you will be able to cope better if you are in a secure and loving relationship.

It Takes Two

At a recent speech I gave on Valentine's Day to a large group of couples, the individual who introduced me asked the audience the question, "How many of you men dragged your wives to this presentation?" The audience laughed while only about 5 percent of the men raised their hand. The problem with this response is that it isn't funny. What it meant was that one partner, in this case the female companion, had to convince the other to attend an evening celebrating their relationship. This one-sidedness troubles me. Too many times I have had a concerned call from a partner asking what they could do to convince their partner to work on the relationship. Sadly, it is usually a female caller. Come on guys, wake up. This is your own well-being and survival we're talking about. Why is it that many of you wait until your partner threatens to leave you before you show any willingness to work on your problems?

The reality of the situation is that it is often the partner who depends on the relationship the most who does the least to keep it strong and healthy. Just look at the statistics of older men who die soon after their female partner dies, and you will realize how much men depend on their partner for their very survival.

Before you begin to think that I'm blaming the male species for all the relationship problems, I want to make it clear that I believe both partners need to take responsibility. A partnership means an alliance, a co-operative union where the partners work together towards a common goal. Unfortunately, sometimes our goals are very different. Willard Gaylin, in his book *Rediscovering Love,* describes his experience as a practicing psychiatrist. He says, "Issues of love and loneliness are still the dominant forces driving women to treatment; problems of work more often motivate male patients. Work and its rewards have become in great part the substitutes for love and relationships in the support of the male ego."

Perhaps the problem lies in our life experiences. After all, we

learned our relationship skills from the families in which we grew up. Those of us who are older are more likely to have grown up in a family environment where roles were clearly defined—roles that expected women to be caregivers at home, while men were responsible for providing the income to sustain the home. It was also expected that a husband and wife stayed together no matter what. Learning skills to improve a marriage was not the norm; you simply accepted your lot in life and developed or relied on other relationships to keep you sane. Divorce was not an option.

In today's world, the opposite is often the case. Statistics show that in the early 1900s, 10 percent of American marriages ended in divorce. Compare that to the divorce rate of 50 percent for couples who were married just seventy years later, and the incredible 67 percent projected for those who married after 1990. If you are interested in finding out more about the climbing divorce rate, I suggest you read John Gottman's book *What Predicts Divorce?*

Perhaps some of us have decided we are never going to experience the pain or loneliness our parents experienced in their relationship, so we have created disposable relationships. If things get tough or don't seem to be working out, we just walk out and look for a new one. The result, unfortunately, is often the same, and the pattern repeats itself. Unless we put in the effort to build a strong and loving relationship, we will continue to experience loneliness.

The statistics look bleak. Even though I am seeing some healthy changes among younger couples and among some partners who are in a second marriage, divorce statistics are still discouraging. As Dr. Gottman points out in another book, *The Seven Principles for Making Marriage Work*, "Half of all divorces will occur in the first seven years. Some studies find that the divorce rate for second marriages is as much as 10 percent higher than for first-timers." You would think that people who are in second marriages would be much more willing to resolve any problems with their relationships.

Fortunately, some of us learn from our mistakes. Susan and I count ourselves as one of those couples. The rewards are great. Once you realize how good a true partnership feels—where two people are genuinely concerned for each other—you may wish you had experienced this type of caring sooner. Unfortunately, too often we don't recognize the true value of a loving relationship until it is too late. The pain and suffering caused by these breakups is immeasurable. So, do yourself a favor and put in the effort.

Do not take your relationship lightly as so many people have. Care for your relationship and it will care for you.

Caring for Your Partner

True love means being concerned for, and interested in, the one you love. Once you can stop being concerned about your own fulfillment, and focus on your partner's needs, you will truly understand what is meant by the sayings: "Love comes back when you give it away" and "Give and you shall receive." Perhaps we need to remind ourselves, as these sayings do, that love is simply a matter of honestly wanting to give your partner those things that mean the most to them. It means giving and caring without expecting a repayment or demanding a return.

Caring for your partner is also a very loving thing to do for yourself. Yes, you read it right, I said *for yourself*. Think about it. Remember the last time you gave a gift to someone, and they were really happy when you gave them this gift. You could see and feel that they really appreciated the thought, the effort, and the gift itself. How did you feel? I'll bet you felt pretty good. The actual act of giving, of caring for someone, felt good for you. So you see, you both benefited from this caring act.

Now you might say this is a very selfish way to look at caring. And you would be right. Yet, sometimes it takes the very act of

feeling good about giving, to motivate a person to continue this behavior. You have to realize, however, that this is a limiting way to care. Caring for your partner only in the hope of being cared for yourself will lead to disappointment. You can only say you truly care when you stop being concerned with yourself, and you begin to be concerned only for your partner. Understand that spending your time and energy in the pursuit of your own happiness and fulfillment will only lead to failure. Human happiness and fulfillment can only be found when we are genuinely concerned for the happiness and fulfillment of others.

Imagine the power, and the effect on your relationship, if you both made a conscious effort to care for each other.

The Partner Who Thought He Cared

Unfortunately, the negative experience of not getting what we want, and not feeling pleasure from what we give, can occur even in a loving relationship. Partners sometimes give things to each other that are not desired or appreciated. This leaves them dissatisfied and wondering if their partner really cares.

Take the case of Troy and Karen. Troy was what you would call a traditional man. He believed a man's role was to look after and protect a woman. Karen had reinforced this role during the early years of their marriage when she had expressed her delight at Troy's success and the financial security that came with it.

Like many men today, Troy felt the need to fulfill this traditional role, and would have considered himself a failure if he could not live up to this expectation. He thought of himself as a caring partner, concerned for Karen's welfare. He strongly believed that providing for Karen's financial security and high standard of living was the best way to show his caring. Imagine his shock and surprise when, after eleven years of marriage, Karen expressed her disappointment.

Karen suggested that he didn't really care for her. She insisted, "He says he loves me, and that he cares, but he really doesn't. He's never home." With pain visible in his eyes, Troy replied angrily, "I don't understand her. I work all day, and sometimes late into the evening and even weekends, to provide for her. She always talked about how important a house and security was to her. She used to be proud of me, and the things I did. Now that we have the house she always wanted, and the comfortable lifestyle, which I seldom get to enjoy, all she does is complain. I don't know what else I can give her." Not surprisingly, Karen was not happy with Troy's grievance over the situation. She responded in a somewhat angry tone, "Sometimes I think you care more about your job than you do about me!"

After a series of attacks and counterattacks, Troy and Karen were eventually able to express what they were really feeling. They both began to realize that what they were upset about was the loss of the companionship and closeness they had experienced during the beginning years of their marriage. With tears in her eyes, Karen talked about her sadness at losing a close companion. She looked directly at Troy and said, "I know how hard you work, and I know you mean well, but I'd give up our house in a flash if we could spend more time together like we used to. The lifestyle is nice, but it's not a life if we can't share it together."

Troy is like many men and women, who confuse a high standard of living with quality of life. Striving to be successful at work is good as long as it doesn't take away from your ability to nurture your relationship. Unfortunately, I have met many couples that get caught up in the pursuit of a high standard of living, mistakenly thinking that they will finally be happy when they achieve their goal.

Now please don't think I'm suggesting that it is wrong to want to be successful or to pursue a higher standard of living. I am suggesting that you must communicate with your partner. As in a true partnership, check in with each other along the way. Make sure that you

express what you really want, and that you are giving to your partner what is desired and appreciated. Sometimes what is wanted is not a big or elaborate gift. Just a single rose or a small teddy bear, for example, can be the ideal gift for your partner. I can't recall how many times couples have shared with me that the simplest gifts were often the most meaningful and cherished. In Chapter 6: Creativity, I will reveal some examples of these appreciated gifts.

In many cases, a meaningful gift doesn't require any *thing* at all. A show of affection—a loving kiss, a warm and tender hug, or the words "I love you"—is often a greater gift than anything you can buy. Remember, simple yet meaningful gestures convey love. They don't need to be expensive or, indeed, cost anything at all. The only requirement is that they are desired. As in the case of Karen and Troy, just spending some quality time together is often all that is needed.

The actual act of caring works best when you have made the effort to discover what would really please the other person.

Knowing what your partner likes and what is meaningful to them, will result in both of you gaining pleasure from the act of caring. You will bring joy to your relationship.

The Ability to Care

By now you are probably thinking, "Okay, I understand the benefits of a caring relationship. I even accept that it takes two. However, caring for my partner without expecting anything in return is not that easy." And you know something? You are right. It isn't easy for most of us. Often we are trying to find someone to love us because we are needy. We are needy because we did not get enough of this love when we were young. As a result we feel empty inside, and we are searching for someone to give to us what someone else could not supply.

The truth is, if you want love in your life, you have to be able to give it to yourself first.

Whenever I give a speech about caring, I always ask the audience: "Did any of you receive unconditional love while you were growing up?" The number of people who raise their hands is usually very small. Not many of us can lay claim to having had the kind of parents who had the ability to nurture and care for us without conditions. As a result, most of us had to learn to develop the ability to love and care for not only someone else but ourselves as well. Jess Lair, in his book *I Ain't Much, Baby—But I'm All I've Got,* describes the fate of most of us when he says, "My God, I didn't get the love that I needed....You're screaming at me for love and, hell, I haven't got anything to give you. I'm so dying to be held and loved and stroked and caressed that I cannot stand it. And yet I'm supposed to give you something that I never got anywhere near enough of. I don't know how to give it."

So, is there hope for those of us who never got enough? The answer is "Yes!" I believe that all of us have some capacity to love. Perhaps that capacity came from the one time we did get some unconditional love—the time we were totally dependent, as a tiny and innocent baby. I was recently reminded of that time when Susan and I were caring for our three grandchildren. The twins Emily and Mackenzie were just tiny babies, while Sarah had reached the ripe old age of 18 months. It didn't seem to matter what Emily, Mackenzie or Sarah did, I always found it cute or adorable. They could drool on me, spill stuff on my clothes and even break things; I loved them just the same. I actually found it easy to give them unconditional love.

The good news is that, for that brief and helpless time of our lives, most of us received some of that love and nurturing so important for our healthy development. We just need to build on the capacity we have. Even if we start with caring just a little, we will get back a little.

So you see, I am not suggesting that only individuals who have overcome dependency, and have the ability to give unconditionally, should enter into a loving relationship. In fact, I am suggesting that a nurturing and caring relationship will contribute to the growth and development of the individuals *in* the relationship. The responsibility for growth, however, lies with the individuals.

Learn how to love yourself, and let yourself be loved. Accept that you have a need to be loved that will probably never be fully satisfied. However, together as partners, you can help each other to become more loving and giving.

A loving relationship is one that promotes individual growth and the capacity to care.

My Own Journey

I have been fortunate to experience this growth and development first-hand. Over the years I have gotten better at being able to care, as well as learn what caring for someone else really means. However, my own journey towards developing the capacity to unselfishly care for another person has been a long one. Actually, this capacity still fails me at times, yet thankfully less and less. As my own loving relationship has grown stronger and healthier, I have developed a greater sense of self-worth and have grown stronger as an individual.

This particular journey started about twenty-five years ago. It began a year after my first marriage ended. As I said earlier, it took a failure to help me learn how to be part of a successful relationship. During my first marriage, I was often not capable of giving because my own needs were so strong. I had not yet acquired the ability to truly care for someone else. My own development as a person had not yet reached the point where I could give without expecting something in return. Yet, here I was, a single parent trying to raise an

11-year-old son, who at times was more capable of giving than I was. I was involved in a series of short-term and failed relationships. My self-esteem was pretty low, and I was beginning to wonder if I would ever meet someone who would love me. Then I met Susan.

I still remember the first time I saw her. She took my breath away. I had just entered a dance club, a club that had a reputation as a good place to meet a companion, when I laid eyes on this gorgeous creature. She was the only person I could focus on. That's when I started to panic. I thought, "How am I going to get up the nerve to ask this beauty to dance? She'll never say 'yes'." To this day I still don't know how my feet started to move and how the words actually came out. I experienced both relief and fear as she responded with a firm "Yes!" Thankfully, she made me feel at ease. That night we danced with no one else but each other, and then spent the rest of the evening talking. Before we knew it, the sun was coming up.

This blooming relationship was magical to me. However, I was focused on getting her to like me, and I experienced fear whenever I thought she might reject me. So you see, I was really into wanting. When it came to being in a relationship, I seemed to be capable of giving only if I got something back in return. I *needed* love more than I was able to give it.

It was also around this time that I decided to return to school. I was 32 years old. Having tried my hand at a number of different careers, successful but not enjoyable, I received some career counseling and completed some assessment tests. That's when I discovered I really wanted to be in some kind of helping profession. I had a strong desire to help others. The capacity to nurture and care for another unconditionally may not have been there, but the desire certainly was. I became passionate about learning the skills to do it well.

I entered a full-time, four-year program to complete a bachelor's degree in psychiatric social work. Later I would continue for an additional five years, part-time, to finish a master's degree in adult education with a specialty in counseling. The good news was that

while I was learning to help others, I was required to learn how to help myself. I was also fortunate to work with some excellent counselors, and was exposed to some great therapeutic experiences. The bad news was that my self-development and constant changing made a mess of my relationship with Susan. We broke up four times during a period of four years. The last breakup happened when I decided I needed to be on my own to "find myself." It lasted for almost a year. I went to live in a small bachelor apartment, while my son Michael went to live with his mom, and Susan found another place. In hindsight, I may have been better off to do my growing up with Susan's support, but I was just too stubborn in those days.

I must admit, however, I did a lot of growing up during that year. I discovered the truth about longing to be loved yet never being satisfied. As John Powell said in his book *Why Am I Afraid to Love?*, "Most of us know our need to be loved and try to seek the love that we need from others. But the paradox remains unresolved; if we *seek* the love, which we need, we will *never find it*. We are lost."

I began to realize that I needed to look inside, and give to myself first the love I so desperately needed. With the help of some excellent counselors and friends, I began my inner journey: a journey that led to a greater acceptance of myself, and to discovering an inner strength that sparked my capacity to love.

I also found myself unable to forget Susan. So one night, I called her up, and asked her if there was any way we could get back together. During this very emotional conversation, I told her that I had come to my senses, and that I believed I had developed enough strength to make our relationship work. I then asked her what it would take for her to believe that I was serious about wanting to make it work. She responded with a question: "How will I know that this time it will work?" I understood that what she really wanted was some proof that I was committed to making it work. Now, you have to realize at this time I was a poor student trying to figure out how I was going to pay back my student loans. That night, however,

I went to the nearest pawnshop and bought her a diamond ring. The next day I showed up on her doorstep, hoping she'd take me back. We were married six months later.

Fortunately I had developed enough capacity to care. I had found the inner strength, the inner love to give of myself. Together we have been able to build a loving relationship, a relationship that has gotten stronger and healthier with each passing year.

Pretending to Care

In my practice I have come across some individuals that I've come to call *placebo carers.* Now you're probably wondering, "What the heck is that?" In the medical profession, a placebo is sometimes given to a patient as a medication, but in reality it is only made up of sugar and water. It's a fake. The interesting thing is that psychologists have discovered that if patients believe they are taking the real medication, the placebo can have a very powerful effect.

For me, the interesting thing is where the word placebo came from and what it actually means. In Latin, placebo means "I shall be pleasing." That's how I coined the term *placebo carer.* Some people pretend to care, to please others, but they are really fakes. They use all the right words and even behave as if they care. They have decided to care, and to be pleasing, in order to receive what they so desperately want: to be loved. They believe in the words: "You're nobody till somebody loves you." The sad part is that too often the recipient of this phony pleaser believes that it's real, at least for a time. Eventually, after experiencing emptiness in their relationship, they begin to realize it's just sugar and water, and not the elixir of true love.

If you identify with this description, remember that developing the capacity to care unconditionally for another person can take a lifetime. You may not have experienced the kind of caring or love

necessary to develop this ability yourself. So you are lacking. That does not mean that you should give up and not even try to develop the strength to care. It is my firm belief that a close relationship is a necessary ingredient in the development of this ability to care. The answer lies in the two of you revealing your inner fears and desires. Be open and honest about your ability to love.

The answer also lies in being genuine. No matter how small your capacity, a little can go a long way. Make a commitment and give what you can, and you will discover that your ability will grow. Before you know it, you will experience a loving relationship in which you are caring and being cared for. It will be real and you will no longer feel alone.

Conditional Caring

Have you ever found yourself placing conditions on your caring? Let's face it, at one time or another we probably all have. For most of us, the road to being able to care for our partner, no matter what, is a long one. More than likely you have placed some of the following conditions on your caring for your partner:

"I will care for you as long as you care for me."
"I will care for you if you do what I say."
"I will care for you again as soon as you apologize."
"I will care for you when you change."

The problem with these kinds of conditions, any conditions on caring for that matter, is that they threaten the health of your relationship. **Threatening to withhold caring is simply not a caring thing to do.** By placing these expectations you are actually showing a lack of caring. You might as well accept that what you are really saying is, "I need you to care for me first before I can care for you."

This admission may be necessary for you to share with each other in order for you to grow and develop as caring partners. Accepting responsibility and self-awareness are important steps in the formation of a loving relationship. As I described earlier, few of us received the kind of nurturing and unconditional love that left us with the strength to care for our partner no matter what the circumstances. However, there is hope. Every time you find the strength to care for your partner, without placing conditions, you are contributing to your own growth. You are also taking another step towards a healthier relationship.

Caring Too Much

Is it possible to care too much? The answer is "yes." Sometimes we grow up believing that we are only good enough if we please others first. We feel driven to help others, yet we are reluctant to ask for anything for ourselves. The problem with this kind of caring, without caring for yourself first, is that it can have a smothering effect on your relationship. Your partner can also start to resent this kind of attention.

Julia was this kind of pleaser. She came for counseling because she was suffering from burnout. No matter how much she gave, she never felt it was enough. Eventually, she felt she couldn't give any more. It became clear during the session that she was driven to make her partner, Mike, happy. Her behavior also spilled over into her work environment, where she always did her best to please everyone. If anyone showed displeasure with her, she would become anxious and concerned, and would try to please even more. No matter how hard she tried, she never felt it was enough. She found herself constantly checking to make sure she was doing the right things. She was looking for assurance. At home, Julia's lack of self-confidence and self-esteem resulted in her alienating the very person she was trying to please.

I performed a simple test, one I had used for many years, to determine whether Julia was suffering from the "caring too much" syndrome. It went as follows: "Julia, imagine you and Mike are passengers on an airplane. You are on your way for a nice relaxing vacation, and suddenly something goes wrong. The plane starts to shake and the cabin pressure begins to drop. The emergency oxygen masks drop from the compartments above. As you scramble for your mask, so that you may breathe, you notice that Mike's oxygen mask failed to drop down. There is no life-saving mask for him to grab. You have a dilemma. Who do you place the oxygen mask on first? Mike, or yourself?" Julia immediately responded, "Mike, of course!"

I'm sure some of you readers would have made the same choice. If that was your answer, you may not know that emergency procedures are very clear. They explicitly advise you to place the mask *on yourself first*, before assisting anyone else. If you are gasping for air while trying to assist another person, there is a likelihood that both of you will die. The same survival procedure is taught to scuba divers. They are told, "when assisting a diver who has run out of air, make sure you give yourself air first, before passing your breathing apparatus to the other diver." The lesson is, have a healthy self-interest. You'll both have a better chance of survival.

In Julia's case, she based her self-esteem on what others thought of her. Her family experiences had led her to believe that she did not deserve love unless she got approval. Approval, in her experience, came only when she was pleasing and being nice. This need for approval was so strong it eventually interfered with her ability to cope. She described her tendency to "constantly ask Mike if he needed anything. Then he would get upset with me and say that I'm smothering him. It didn't matter what I did; it was never right. I don't know what to do anymore."

The relationship between Mike and Julia had been deteriorating for some time. When I asked them what had attracted them to each other, I received a very familiar response. I say familiar because I have found that we are usually attracted to people who have about the same level of self-esteem as we do ourselves. In both of their cases, self-esteem was pretty low. Yet, as is usual, they did not reveal their inner fears to each other. Instead, they tried to act strong and self-confident. Mike came across as a strong and considerate person, while Julia acted self-assured and outgoing. As Mike said, "She was so nice to everyone. So caring." Julia, on the other hand, was attracted to the strength displayed by Mike. "I really believed he would take care of me." The problem was that the behavior they showed to the outside world was very different from their internal experience. Inside, they both felt scared and unsure. Unfortunately, the very person they believed would give them what they needed, was not real. Julia and Mike had fallen for a false image. After three years of marriage, they were disillusioned and disappointed.

What saved their relationship was the love they still had for each other. Deep down, they genuinely cared and wanted to make it work. Eventually they were able to share their true fears with each other. The experience of being accepted for who they really were by the partner they loved, was extremely healing. They were able to build on their capacity to love and, in effect, heal themselves.

I continue to be amazed by the power of healing relationships. Caring relationships, where each partner is concerned for the other, can help individuals learn to heal themselves.

Caring and Children

I want to ask a couple of questions of those of you who have very young children. How is your intimate relationship? Are you taking time together for just the two of you, without the children? If your answer is that you are too busy and will have to wait until the

children are older, I urge you to reconsider that decision. I am making this appeal because too often young parents develop serious relationship problems when they neglect each other.

In case you are concerned that your children will suffer if you pay more attention to your partner, think again. After all, just as you were affected by the family environment you grew up in, so too are your children. You are modeling the relationship they will consider to be normal. So what do you want them to experience? A home where both parents are doing everything for them, but do not seem to spend much time caring for each other? Or the kind of loving home, where everyone is cared for, including the caregivers? I'm sure you chose the second option.

I realize that to achieve this kind of relationship requires some difficult balancing of priorities. I am never suggesting that you rob your children of the kind of love and caring they deserve. Let me rephrase that, the kind of love and caring they need. What I am suggesting is that you don't rob from your own needs. After all, caring for children requires all the energy and abilities at your disposal. I'm sure you often find yourself saying, "I don't have any more to give." All the more reason that you must find ways to replenish your energy and ability to give.

In fact, your moods will have a direct effect on your children's behavior. Have you ever noticed that when you are feeling anxious and tired, your children also seem restless and have difficulty settling down? Yet, when you are well rested and feeling calm, your children are less troubled. These experiences serve as a constant reminder of the positive influence your renewed energy and warmth have on your children's behavior and moods. And the best way to renew your energy and warmth is to take time together, as a couple, and charge your love batteries.

Now before you start thinking, "I don't have the time to replenish my energy. I can't leave them for a minute," think again. Showing love and affection for your partner does not require a lot of time or

energy. A simple hug, holding your partner's hand, or an affectionate kiss can do wonders. It not only replenishes your energy, it is a wonderful experience for your children to be exposed to. Show them what a loving relationship is all about. Who better to act as role models than the very people who love and nurture them, and who brought them into this world? There is no need to starve yourselves of the affection and nurturing you and your children need.

I have to admit that it saddens me to hear individual partners talk about the loneliness they experience because their partners no longer spend any time with them. Even while the primary caregiver may complain about not having any time with other adults, their own partner is neglected. The really sad part in all this is that these loving parents are unaware that they are robbing their children of a loving family—a family where each member is concerned for the well-being of everyone, including themselves.

The greatest gift you can give your children is a loving relationship.

Caring for the Child Within

There is in every one of us, a part that still feels like a child—a child with wants and desires that need to be nourished just as surely as those of our own children. I had had a vague awareness about this phenomenon; however, it wasn't until the early 1970s that I learned a method that helped to make sense of it all. This is a method that I still use today when helping a couple to understand some of their inner drives and needs.

The theory behind this method was actually developed by Dr. Eric Berne. You may remember him as the person who wrote a book that was at the top of the bestseller lists for more than two years. It's called *Games People Play.* In it, Dr. Berne describes how

sometimes we seem to have several different people living inside of us. He calls them ego states. For our purpose, let's look at two of them. One is called the *Parent ego state*; the other is known as the *Child ego state.*

Perhaps the best way I can illustrate this phenomenon is for you to imagine that it's a warm summer day. You walk past your favorite ice cream parlor. Just as you look inside at the customers enjoying their delicious treats, you hear a voice in your head say, "Would I ever love a nice cool ice cream cone right now!" Then you hear another voice, "You're on a diet. And besides, it's too close to dinnertime. You'll spoil your appetite!" What you just heard, inside your head, is the Child and the Parent beginning what will probably be a bit of a debate as to whether or not you are going to go in and treat yourself. This type of conversation goes on inside our heads much of the time. Don't worry, it's normal. It's only when you start doing it out loud, in public, that people might look at you and think you're kind of strange.

The important thing about being aware of these ego states is to know that they affect how we communicate with other people. Imagine, for example, that it had been you and your partner walking past the ice cream parlor, and she had expressed an interest in a nice cool treat, and your response was to tell her, "No! You shouldn't have one. Remember your diet!" Well, I don't need to tell you, you probably already know that she would feel like a little child who had just been scolded by her parent. It might have been a lot better if you had said, "Go for it, hon! A few calories won't hurt. After the day you've had, you deserve a treat." The difference with this exchange is that in the first example you were being critical, while in the second your response was more nurturing and caring. It takes a little extra effort, but believe me, it's worth it.

The problem arises when our inner child feels deprived, and we are not aware of it. Let's say you still crave the nurturing you never got as a young child. If you keep this desire hidden from yourself,

you may just pretend that you don't need it, and play out the "tough independent guy" role. Or you may be very demanding of your partner, and expecting him or her to satisfy your craving for attention. In either case you have a problem. It may be rather difficult for you to provide nurturing to your partner when you yourself are so needy. The danger is that your unreasonable demands and self-defeating behavior may drive away the very person you desire.

The answer, again, lies in healing yourself. Begin by accepting your own deprived inner child and nurturing yourself. Do not expect your partner to fill the void that exists in you. **A loving partner can be supportive, but only you can satisfy your longing.**

Hi Hon, I'm Home

Imagine for a moment, that you are preparing to have a relaxing and enjoyable evening with your partner. You have decided to really please her by preparing her favorite meal. You bought some flowers and put on that shirt she really likes. The anticipation of her arrival is growing. You hear her car drive up, so you stop what you're doing and go to the door to greet her. As you open the door you notice something is wrong. She slams the car door and has a look on her face that is anything but pleasant. She storms past you, grumbling something about "those idiots at work!" What do you do?

Well, for starters, I would not suggest you criticize her for being in a bad mood by saying something like, "You just ruined the wonderful evening I had planned for us." Unfortunately, if you have ever been in this situation, and most of us have, that's probably what came out of your mouth. So what can you do to salvage the evening? Well I have a suggestion. Stop behaving like a critical parent and do what you can to give your partner some support and nurturing. I realize that may be hard to do when you are feeling disappointed and in need of some recognition yourself, especially after all the effort you put into the

evening. Remember the quote I mentioned earlier, "Give and you shall receive." This is a case that can test the validity of this saying.

Here is something you can do. You know she's had a rough day, so more than likely the little child inside her could really use some attention—not critical attention, but the kind of nurturing that soothes and replenishes. After all, you put a lot of effort into preparing for a relaxing and enjoyable evening; just a little more effort isn't going to hurt. Understand that some real caring right now would really be appreciated by her. So appreciated, in fact, that most likely her bad mood will begin to disappear, and after a short time her inner child will probably want to enjoy the evening as well. She may even want to play. Believe me, that's when the real fun begins.

Acceptance

All of us want to be accepted. This desire to be accepted is strongest in our long-term intimate relationship. As Erica Jong says, "We fall in love with people because somebody knows us for who we are and sticks around."

Imagine being accepted, not for your looks or the car you drive, or the clothes you wear, for none of the external things, but for what's inside you. Imagine someone who really knows us, with all our frailties and failings, and still accepts us for who we are. That's love.

To accept a person who is very different from ourselves can be a challenge. If you truly love them, however, celebrate their uniqueness. Watch and appreciate them as they grow, and reward and recognize them simply for being who they are. This is the greatest gift you can ever give them.

Take, for instance, the effect on children who are labeled as "underachievers" by their teacher—or children who are told they are not good enough, and considered failures by parents. The impact of those messages can last a lifetime. They last because we accept those labels and begin to see ourselves only according to other people's perceptions. Can you remember a person who negatively influenced your self-image? Is that message still influencing you today, or has a loving partner or a caring relationship helped you to change how you see yourself?

My experience has shown that you can release yourself from the various ways you have been labeled by others. In the early years of my training I was, and still am, greatly influenced by the teachings of Dr. Carl Rogers. Dr. Rogers is famous for his non-directive and client-centered system of counseling. His theory supports the concept that the basic challenge and need of every human life is self-understanding, self-acceptance and the drive to reach our full potential. He calls it self-actualization. It is necessary, however, that in order for us as individuals to develop to our full potential, we must first accept ourselves as we are. Dr. Rogers also suggests that it is difficult for us to accept ourselves as we truly are until another has first understood and accepted us for what we are. Acceptance is most powerful when it comes from a loving partner.

I believe in the power of a loving and caring relationship to help us become fully alive and to accept ourselves for who we are. A nurturing relationship can help to turn a negative self-image into a positive one. Strengths will also develop more rapidly, and individuals will more easily reach their full potential in a relationship where both partners are caring and supportive of each other.

Once you have been accepted and loved for who you are, you will be better able to reduce negative influences, and your inner strengths will begin to surface. As your self-acceptance increases, so will your capacity to love. As I stated before, to be able to truly love your partner, you cannot be preoccupied only with yourself. In a loving relationship, both partners are focused on the happiness and fulfillment of the other.

Imagine the power of a relationship where both partners accept each other for who they are.

The Power of Recognition

At the beginning of this section I talked about our biological need to be touched—how necessary it is for our survival and well-being. There is another need that you should be aware of. It is the psychological need to be recognized. The need for recognition can be just as strong as the need for physical contact.

As we grow older, the psychological need for recognition stays with us and remains strong. When was the last time you went to a retirement home and talked to some of the residents? Did you notice their faces when you talked to them, or gave them a smile? As Leo Buscaglia once said, "Nearly every one of us is starving to be appreciated." No wonder we live in a world where low self-esteem is the norm.

It is a well-known fact that we need to be recognized by the important people in our lives in order to develop a strong feeling of self-worth. It is the power of recognition that determines how we feel about ourselves. How we were treated and recognized by our parents, teachers, or any of the people who cared for us during our younger years, can have a profound effect on how we react and behave with our loving partner. Therefore, if you received lots of hugs and affection, as well as caring compliments, you are likely to be very comfortable with receiving and giving similar recognition. Being exposed to statements like, "I'm really glad you're my son," or "I'm proud to call you my daughter," serves to boost our own capacity to care and give similar compliments to the ones we love.

Just reflect for a moment on a time when a loving parent gave you a genuine and appropriate compliment, a smile, or a word of praise. How did you feel? I'm sure you felt great. Some of you may have acted embarrassed on the outside, while on the inside you felt as if you had been given a gift. It might have felt as if you just received a boost of energy. Perhaps the air in your lungs seemed to expand and you stood a little straighter. A feeling of pride may have come over you. Don't you wish you could experience those moments more often?

Now imagine that the person giving you this compliment is your loving partner. You hear them say, "You're such a wonderful person to be with," or "I'm so proud of you." If you often receive this kind of recognition from your partner, then I don't have to tell you how good it feels, or how it affects your very soul. Regardless of the amount and type of recognition you received growing up, the experience of receiving a loving compliment will still heal and nurture you.

Here is your chance to experience a nurturing moment first-hand. Instead of me sharing another case history about how other couples show their healing recognition, I suggest you engage in the following exercise. It will only take you fifteen minutes, but the benefits will last for days, weeks, even months. Mark Twain is reported to have said that he could go for two months on a good compliment. Believe me, it is time well invested.

1. Select a quiet place with few distractions.
2. Sit facing your partner, and look into each other's eyes.
3. Take turns sharing a loving compliment with each other. Tell your partner something you appreciate about them, or something they've done, or simply express your affection (a genuine "I love you" is always nice).
4. Watch your partner's reaction. Be aware of how you feel, and your feelings towards your partner, as you engage in this nurturing moment.
5. When you have finished this exercise, share your experience with each other.

Recognition contributes tremendously to the health and strength of your relationship. It can also have a lasting effect.

The expression of affection and appreciation is such a wonderful gift. Give it often.

What's Your Caring IQ? (Me)

The following exercise will help you to rate your caring behavior, and determine how much effort you are putting into your relationship. After reading each question, give yourself a score of one to five. When you finish, add up your score and review the results with your partner.

Never		Sometimes		Always
1	2	3	4	5

Do you give your partner warm and loving hugs? ______
Do you hold hands in public? ______
Do you kiss your partner affectionately before you leave the house? ______
Do you stop what you're doing and inquire about your partner's day, and show a genuine interest? ______
Do you play and have fun with your partner? ______
Do you compliment your partner? ______
Do you show your appreciation and say "I love you"? ______
Do you celebrate milestones (anniversaries, birthdays, the day you first met)? ______
Do you give your partner special gifts on days when they are not expected? ______
Do you go to a romantic movie, or watch a video together? ______
Do you set aside "quality time" to focus on each other? ______
Do you take time to discuss, review and tell each other what you want from your relationship? ______

Total Points

Enter your total score here: ______

What's Your Caring IQ? (Partner)

After reading each question, give yourself a score of one to five. When you finish, add up your score and review the results with your partner.

Never		Sometimes		Always
1	2	3	4	5

Do you give your partner warm and loving hugs? _______
Do you hold hands in public? _______
Do you kiss your partner affectionately before you leave the house? _______
Do you stop what you're doing and inquire about your partner's day, and show a genuine interest? _______
Do you play and have fun with your partner? _______
Do you compliment your partner? _______
Do you show your appreciation and say "I love you"? _______
Do you celebrate milestones (anniversaries, birthdays, the day you first met)? _______
Do you give your partner special gifts on days when they are not expected? _______
Do you go to a romantic movie, or watch a video together? _______
Do you set aside "quality time" to focus on each other? _______
Do you take time to discuss, review and tell each other what you want from your relationship? _______

Total Points

Enter your total score here: _______

Results

40 or above: Congratulations. You are a caring partner who shows a genuine interest in the well-being of your partner and your relationship. Continue to practice these caring behaviors and your relationship will grow stronger and remain healthy. You will also improve your own emotional and physical health, helping you to increase the time you will spend together as a caring and loving couple.

Below 40: Discuss with your partner what caring behaviors you do easily. Find out what other caring acts would be appreciated, and determine which of these you would be willing to practice. Every time you increase your caring behavior you are improving your relationship. Care for your partner and your relationship, and you will be cared for.

Add your own: There may be other caring things you do for your partner that are not described in the previous exercise. Discuss these with your partner and decide whether or not they qualify. Any legitimate caring behavior will make your relationship better. Feel free to list these caring behaviors below. Score these caring examples and add the points to your results.

My own caring examples:

____

____

____

____

My partner's caring examples:

____

____

____

____

Reflect

Reflect on your ability to care. Can you remember those times when you were cared for, and how this experience affected you? Think about your relationship and how your caring behavior affects the relationship *and* yourself. Are you able to care for your partner, even during those times when your partner is not able to care for you?

What do you need to do to become a more caring person? Are you taking responsibility for the strength and health of your relationship? Jot down a few notes about what you can do, and what you want.

Me

My Partner

A Beautiful Balance

Sometimes you give and I receive, and sometimes I give and you receive, and sometimes we both give. It is all a beautiful balance. It is a loving partnership where two people, who have developed the ability to care for themselves, and each other, come together and grow together.

Make a commitment to care for your partner, for your relationship and for yourself. List these caring behaviors in the space below. In order to make sure that these caring acts are well received, discuss them with your loving partner. Choose what you consider to be the most important caring behavior for a healthy relationship. Transfer this choice to your self-contract at the end of this book.

Me

____

____

____

____

____

____

____

____

My Partner

____

____

____

____

____

____

____

____

Change

The most loving thing you can do for your relationship is to accept your partner as he or she really is.

The Expectation

"If only you would change, we would have a great relationship!"

Many people come for counseling believing that their partner is responsible for the problems in their relationship. The request for change is often driven by a strong desire to have a better relationship. And so the request for change is legitimate. However, how we make this request is very important. Too often we criticize our partner. We find fault with their behavior, challenge their choices and too quickly show our displeasure. We treat our partners as if they were a home improvement project. It is as if we are trying to create the ideal person. That strategy may work in a fictional world, but not in the one in which we live.

Speaking about fiction, I was recently watching a science fiction program called *Star Trek Voyager*. In one scene, the captain, Katherine

Janeway, has fallen in love with a hologram (a computer-generated being). As she discussed her desire to change her lover with the ship's doctor (also a hologram), he commented on the tendency of human beings to try to change the people with whom they fall in love. Janeway's response perhaps reflects the secret desire of a great many people. She said, "He's exactly my type. Attractive, intelligent, we share the same interests, and if there is something I don't like, I can simply change it."

How many of you wish your partner were a simple program that you could reprogram at your whim? Well, if you actually got your wish, you might be very disappointed with the result. The illusion that we know what's best for our partner can be destructive—destructive in that it can stop our partner from developing their own uniqueness. What a loss that would be. The reality is that we can be no one as well as we can be ourselves. Also, the only person who can truly change us is ourself, and then only when we want to change.

You cannot change another person without his or her permission.

Sadly, some of us believe that we have the right to decide how another person should be. I must admit that during the formative years of my relationship with Susan, I made several attempts to try to change her. "After all," I believed, "I'm in training to be a psychotherapist, and I'm making changes to myself, so why shouldn't she?" Naturally, my attempts were met with a lot of resistance. I don't think she ever read any book I recommended to her; however, she did read many books she acquired for herself. So here I was, in training, and learning that the only behavior you can change is your own, yet I wasn't applying it in my own loving relationship. Talk about a slow learner.

It is important to remember that the responsibility for growth and change is *your* responsibility. Likewise, you must allow your partner to develop, at his or her own pace, into the unique person they were meant to be.

Why Change?

The answer to that question is that change is inevitable. In fact, if you want a healthy relationship, you have to be willing to allow it to develop and grow, and that means change. Without change there is no growth; the relationship will get stale and eventually die.

You could compare a relationship to a plant. A plant that is nurtured will grow and change, and will develop into the beautiful creation it is meant to be. Just like a plant, your relationship is a living thing, and as it is nurtured so will it grow and change.

We also know that a healthy plant can help to keep our air clean, resulting in a healthier environment for the humans around it. The same is true for a healthy relationship: everyone around two loving partners will benefit.

Therefore, please allow your partner to be free, and to develop into the person they were meant to be. If you truly love them, celebrate and accept their uniqueness. As John O'Donohue once said, "The magic of change is the contented heart."

Watch and appreciate your partner as they grow, and reward and recognize them simply for who and what they are. This is the greatest gift you can ever give them.

The Pain of Changing

The fact remains that for most of us, change is not easy. For years, I have been stating the following truism: "When the pain of changing becomes less than the pain of staying the same, people will change." I say this as a reminder that most of us will continue to resist change. It is only when the situation becomes too painful that we begin to accept the fact that we would be better off if we did change. Sometimes, we may have wanted a change in our relationship, but

we haven't done anything about it because we are afraid. We are afraid of the unknown, and prefer the familiar. How many people do you know, including yourself, who are in situations that are unpleasant? They remain stuck because they fear that the effort required to make the change is more painful than where they are. It is not until the situation gets too painful that they are motivated to change.

So you see, change can happen if a situation becomes too painful. Wouldn't it be better, though, if we were motivated to change because the experience led to more joy? Then we would say, "When the pleasure of changing became greater than the pleasure of staying the same, we would welcome the change." Whether we define change as easy or hard, it is necessary.

In order for your relationship to bloom and remain healthy, it must be nurtured and encouraged to change and to develop.

Opposites Attract

Have you ever noticed how often people who seem very different from each other enter into an intimate, long-term relationship? It has been said that romance is borne out of differences, as well as similarities. The unexpected can excite us, yet we also long for the familiar. Eventually the longing for the familiar can become stronger. We find ourselves saying, "If only he/she were more like me, we'd get along better!" Perhaps you are one of these couples. The irony is that we spend most of our lives looking for our "other half," and when we find that person, we work hard at trying to mould them into a copy of ourselves.

We seem to forget that we were attracted to the uniqueness and difference of our life partner. It was, in fact, this difference in personality and behavior that excited us and made our hearts pound. It is also the balance of these differences that often makes a great partnership.

For example, if you are the type of person who is restrained and cautious, you might be attracted to a person who is daring and adventuresome, and who likes to take risks. On the other hand, if you are impulsive and emotional you are likely to be attracted to a partner who is serene and predictable.

I also believe, however, that the basic core values and the likes and dislikes of any two partners should be similar. For example, Susan and I are similar in our moral beliefs, sexual attraction, emotional connection, family commitments and taste in pleasures like travel, music and food. Our core similarities have helped us to see eye to eye on many occasions.

On the other hand, our behavioral style is very different. I'm what you would call an introvert. Even though I have made many presentations to large audiences, I feel drained afterwards. I need time alone to recharge my batteries, and I usually sneak off to find some solitude. Susan is the opposite. She's an extrovert, and gets energy from being with people. That explains why at parties she's a perfect hostess, mingling with everyone and making sure they have what they want, while I tend to limit myself to fewer people, engaging in more one-on-one conversations. Over the years, our different behavioral styles have helped to make us a better team, even though they sometimes cause some frustration. It is the blending of our complementary strengths and weaknesses that makes for a great partnership.

The key lies in the balancing of these differences. Too much difference or unpredictability can frighten us. We want to experience a secure attachment and connection. We want to feel safe. And feeling safe can come from a sense of predictability. That's where the challenge lies. Each of us has unique thoughts, feelings and behaviors. The more similar our partner's thoughts, feelings and behaviors are to our own, the easier it is for us to understand our partner.

Understanding our partner makes it easier to trust and connect with them.

All Men Are the Same

Now that I have your attention, let me voice a growing concern of mine. I am concerned about the tendency of some couples to categorize each other as if their behavior is fixed according to their gender. Statements like, "He can't help it. That's the way he is. After all, he's a man." Or "What do you expect? She's a woman. You know they're all too emotional." These couples are making the assumption that all men, and all women, behave in predictable ways. They assume that we behave the way we do because of our gender. Whether we were born this way, or whether we were conditioned to be this way, it doesn't seem to matter. The assumption is that we are all alike and predictable.

When I ask these individuals where they got this notion, the response I often receive is, "From the experts. You just have to read all the books about men and women, and you'll find out how different we are." Occasionally they will even give me direct quotes from these books. One female client recited to me, "It's easier for a man to take off his clothes in front of a woman than to lay bare his soul." I thought that was a pretty good description of *some* men's tendency to have difficulty with expressing their deep inner feelings. However, I did not believe the author meant to say that all men are like that! So I asked my client to bring in this book. It turns out she was quoting from a book called, *The Trouble With You*, written by Zelda West-Meads. I had a chance to read it and consider it a well-written book. I even went out and bought my own copy. However, as I pointed out to my client, Zelda does not claim that a particular characteristic is solely the preserve of one sex. In fact, Zelda states very clearly that, "There are plenty of aggressive, ambitious (male characteristics) women, and sensitive, caring (female characteristics) men."

Zelda, like other authors, including myself, will often describe tendencies and predominant characteristics of men and women. We understand that a society will influence the behavior of people exposed to its norms. So, yes, there has been a tendency for boys and girls to be raised according to different standards. However, that does not mean we are forever fixed in the way we relate to each other.

What is important is that we accept that these differences exist in both sexes. They are certainly not the exclusive domain of one or the other gender. I am sure you will agree that if someone said they could tell you exactly what kind of person you were by the way you looked, you might be concerned. Unfortunately, we often grow up adopting certain prejudices that color our perceptions. When that happens, we only see what we want to see.

Our perceptions are distorted, and thus we fail to see each other's uniqueness.

Accepting Uniqueness

A great partnership is comprised of a variety of unique strengths and weaknesses. It is actually a great balancing act. However, to be able to accept these differences is not always easy. When our partner's behavioral dimensions are different from our own, we have to work harder to appreciate these differences. Therefore, understanding the uniqueness of our partner, and appreciating how that brings balance to our relationship, will improve communication, reduce conflict, and help to create a healthier relationship.

Accept that your partner is different from you. When you begin to appreciate your partner's individual differences, instead of criticizing them, you have taken an important step towards improving your relationship.

Unfortunately, we tend to think that because someone is different from us, or approaches things differently, they are wrong. We forget

that diversity brings a richness and variety to our relationship that would be sorely missed if we were both the same. Actually, I'd be the first to admit that if I had to live with someone exactly like me, I'm not sure I could take it. Being different does not mean being wrong, it simply means, not the same. However, sometimes dealing with our partner according to their personality type is like trying to speak another language.

You will be able to communicate well with your partner if you learn to "speak their language" by using words, examples and descriptions that they can understand and relate to. Just as you need to speak Italian in Rome to be understood, you need to know how to speak to your partner so that they can understand you. I'm sure you have found yourself feeling frustrated because you couldn't "speak the language." And simply speaking louder did not get you anywhere at all.

It is a loving relationship when two people understand and accept each other's uniqueness.

Same Situation, Different Perceptions

It never ceases to amaze me how often two people can experience the same situation but perceive it very differently. Consider the case of Jim and Linda. Jim is waiting for Linda at a restaurant. Linda is fifteen minutes late for their luncheon date because she has been helping her sister sort through a relationship conflict.

Jim's Perception

After checking his watch for the umpteenth time, Jim begins to experience anger building up inside:

Fifteen minutes already...Linda's late again...Isn't that just like her...She really doesn't care ...Why can't she be more considerate?...Wish I could just show up late whenever I felt like it...but that's not me...not my style...This is getting serious...pretty soon I'll have to be back at work...I'll bet she'll have another great excuse...she always does...I'd better keep my cool though, or this whole lunch will be spoiled again...

"Hey, babe. I have to get back to work soon. I have an important meeting after lunch. I wish you'd call and let me know when you're delayed, so I don't have to sit here waiting."

Linda's Perception

As Linda enters the restaurant, she sees Jim and gives him a wave. With a big smile on her face she walks towards him. She thinks:

Ah, good...Jim hasn't ordered yet...That was really an emotional experience...I wish Joan didn't get upset so easily about Bob's obsession with his hobby...I'm glad I don't have those kind of problems with Jim...Good thing I spent a bit extra time listening though...she seemed pretty calm when I hung up...I'll call her back later to make sure she's okay ...Jim doesn't look too happy...but after all, family is more important than being on time...

"Hi, hon. Sorry to be a little late. Joan was all upset, and I didn't feel I could leave her in that condition. I hope you understand."

Jim is upset because being punctual is important to him. He prides himself on always being on time. Linda, on the other hand, places punctuality somewhat lower on her list of priorities. She believes that people, and especially family, are more important than being on time.

Linda and Jim's life experiences, which shape their perceptions, brought them to their lunch date with different expectations, moti-

vations and perceptions. The same fifteen-minute timespan that seemed an eternity to Jim, seemed insignificant to Linda. While each found the other's actions frustrating, each felt that their own behavior was reasonable and understandable.

Jim's motivation came from his desire to be in control. He prides himself on being direct, decisive and results-oriented. He fears losing control and being taken advantage of. He interpreted Linda's behavior as being inconsiderate, and wonders why Linda seems to think that other people are more important to her than he is. In contrast, Linda's motivation is rooted in her desire to help others and restore peace. The human needs of her sister had priority over the social task of the luncheon date. She found Jim's lack of understanding to be unreasonable. She doesn't understand how Jim sees this as his needs being less important to her than listening to her sister's problems.

Intellectually, we can appreciate that others' views of the world can be very different from our own. Emotionally, however, we may have difficulty acting on that recognition. Like Linda and Jim, we tend to believe that we are right and the other person is wrong. Think about it. As you read this example, who were you siding with? Linda or Jim?

Focus on Strengths

Some couples seem to have a natural ability to build a caring relationship. They focus on what is good in their relationship in order to make it even better. Other couples complain about what is wrong in their relationship, lay guilt trips on each other and keep repeating the same mistakes.

As I said earlier in my introduction, my goal with this book, and through workshops and couple's counseling, is to help couples create a healthy relationship. That process involves helping couples to become more positive and supportive. In my experience, if you and your loving partner want an invincible relationship, the process of making this happen becomes easier when both partners are able to focus on their strengths and learn to manage their weaknesses. One of the best books written about this subject is entitled *Soar With Your Strengths*. The authors, Donald Clifton and Paula Nelson, begin their book with a parable about a rabbit that goes to school so he can be smarter. Over the past couple of years I have used and adapted this parable when speaking to couples about focusing on the behaviors that bring joy to their relationship. With some poetic license, I have adapted the parable here:

There was once a rabbit that went to a school offering courses on how to become a well-rounded animal. The courses include: running, swimming, tree climbing and flying.

In the first course, the rabbit was a star. He felt so good running over the hills and down the valleys as fast as he could go. With his strong muscles in his rear legs he was the fastest in the class. The instructor said that he would be able to run even faster with some training. He felt great.

That night he told his life partner (for this story let's just assume that rabbits have life partners) how much fun school was. She told him how proud she was, and said that he would be an even better partner after he learned all those other skills. They both felt great.

The next day's course concentrated on swimming. The rabbit was told to jump in the water. Being a brave rabbit, he jumped in. Unfortunately, no matter how hard he tried to swim, he kept sinking. The instructor pulled him out just as he was starting to panic. He left school that day a very disheartened and unhappy rabbit.

After sharing his disappointment with his partner, she encouraged him to try again. She told him that she believed in him and that he could do anything he set his mind to. She also made it clear that she wanted him to be successful and to graduate, and that meant completing all the courses.

At this point the rabbit decided to get some help. So he went to see a

coach. After some assessments and testing, the coach announced that he understood the problem. He suggested that since the rabbit could run so very well, he didn't need to take those classes anymore, but he would arrange for him to have more swimming classes.

As soon as he heard that suggestion, the rabbit just threw up!

The moral of this story is that too often you are told you are not good enough unless you change. And change in this case means working on your weaknesses. It may even be suggested that you go for counseling in order to overcome your weaknesses. Unfortunately, if you are focused only on your weaknesses, you will be spending a lot of wasted energy. When you focus on your weaknesses, it begins to suffocate your strengths. Focusing on the failures in your relationship will only make you feel worse, and you will inevitably neglect the successes.

The greatest chance for creating a strong bond and loving relationship with your partner lies in remembering and improving on the positive things, and getting back on track, while doing less of the negative things. Just as Paula and Donald suggest in *Soar With Your Strengths*, "If you develop your strengths to the maximum, the strengths becomes so great they overwhelm the weaknesses."

Instead of thinking about what is wrong with the relationship, identify and develop what is right.

The Invincible Relationship

Many disagreements in a relationship are about not getting enough of something we want from our partner. A typical complaint I have heard from couples concerns the level of affection in their relationship. One partner may nag that the other is not spontaneous, or frequent enough with the amount of hugging and kissing. The other then protests that they are not a "deep-feeling" type of person, and that they never experienced that in their home. So the typical cycle becomes one of complaint about the other's shortcomings. Threats about "improve or face the consequences" begin to fly. Unfortunately, threats to change or improve can overwhelm a person, and will not likely get us the response we are looking for, just as the person who marches up to their partner and aggressively shouts, "Kiss me!" isn't likely to get a warm and affectionate response.

The answer lies in managing the things you don't do well, and discovering and nurturing the things you do best. I am not suggesting that we shouldn't change. I accept that we may need to adjust our behavior. Even if we were raised in an environment where little affection was shown, we can learn to give and receive affection ourselves. However, we can't expect to become a spontaneous and overly affectionate person. Weaknesses cannot be transformed into strengths.

Think about what your relationship would be like if you devoted more time to discovering what you and your partner appreciate and enjoy. Imagine spending most of your time working on the good stuff until the positive experiences simply overwhelm the negative ones.

I just love the story about the Chinese table tennis player during the 1984 Olympics. It seems this particular player had a major weakness. He couldn't play with his backhand, with the result that he played with only his forehand. His competition knew this, so the coaches instructed all their players to go for his backhand. "Get the ball there and you've got him beat. He won't be able to return it!" they said. And so they did. Player after player won a point whenever they shot the ball at his backhand. Unfortunately for them, they just couldn't get the ball to his backhand often enough to make a difference. The Chinese player won the gold medal. You see, he was playing with his strength. When the coach of the

Chinese team was interviewed and asked about his training method, he replied, "We practice eight hours a day perfecting our strengths." He instinctively knew that if his player's strong forehand became even stronger, it would overwhelm his weak backhand.

Imagine what counseling would be like if you came in and started telling me what was right with your relationship, and stated that you were there specifically to learn how to make it even better. I guess now you know why the slogan on my Web page states: "Helping to make good relationships even better!"

The answer lies in discovering and nurturing those things you do best, while managing the things you don't do well.

If you want an invincible relationship, one that cannot be beaten, then focus on and develop your individual strengths.

Help Me to Understand

Research evidence supports the conclusion that the most satisfied partners are those who know themselves, recognize the demands of the situation and adapt strategies to meet those needs. Most of us find it easier to see things from our own perspective. We find it more difficult to see things from another person's point of view. That is the challenge that you need to accept. You do need to understand yourself; however, you also need to understand your partner and try to see things differently. By being able to see things differently and being aware of a variety of points of view, you will be able to make a better connection with your partner and create a better relationship.

Over the years, I have searched for different ways to help couples understand and appreciate their unique differences. If couples don't understand these unique differences between them, it can lead to frustration and confusion, often causing one or both part-

ners to accuse the other one of being unreasonable. One of the methods that I have found to be very effective in correcting this is to administer one of several behavioral-style assessment tools. I refer to them as awareness tools. Properly applied and interpreted, these tools can help us to better understand ourselves and others. They are designed to identify our predictable patterns of behavior, and to describe what, how, and even why we do the things we do. Understanding your partner's point of view will often help to bring your differences out into the open and defuse potential problems. At the very least, you will finally understand why certain things your partner does seem to bug you more than you'd like.

DiSC® Dimensions of Behavior

The awareness tools that I use most often in my counseling practice are called the *DiSC® Relationship Profile*, the *Personal Profile System®* and the *Personal Listening Profile®*. Certainly, there are other popular awareness tools, like the *Myers Briggs Type Indicator®*, which I occasionally use as well. However, the *Profile* instruments are usually very good at providing insights about your own unique behavioral pattern and that of your partner. They also provide information on how to strengthen your relationship by identifying and understanding the behavioral needs of your partner.

The *DiSC® Profiles*, developed by Dr. John Geier and Carlson Learning Company, are unique and powerful tools. They are easy to understand and provide enough information to aid you, the respondent, in interpreting the results. The uniqueness of the *Profiles* is that you are considered to be the expert on yourself. You do not have to be a trained psychologist to use these tools. The instruments are self-administered, self-scored and self-interpreted. This self-approach has made the *DiSC Profiles* easy to use for anyone who wants to learn more about themselves or their relationship.

Strengthening Your Relationship

Each of us is a unique blend of the four *DiSC*® behavioral styles or dimensions. They are: **D***ominance,* **i***nfluence,* **S***teadiness* and **C***onscientiousness* (DiSC). The *Personal Profile System*® identifies fifteen most commonly occurring behavioral patterns, or "classical profile patterns."

Understanding your personality style and identifying your behavioral pattern can help you be more aware of your patterns of behavior, and can help you learn to act more appropriately and effectively in any situation. Let's look at the various behavioral patterns so that you can identify which type you resemble. Then we will look at how you can adjust and adapt your unique style to create a more secure bond with your partner. See if you can identify your style as you read through the following illustrations.

The "D" Type Personalities

These are the "let's get it done" types. They are the **drivers** and the **doers**. "D"s are very demanding and have difficulty taking "no" for an answer. They are inquisitive and self-assured. They know what they want and go after it. They like to take charge.

If this snapshot description fits you or your partner's style, review the following four profile patterns listed below, and see if you can find an even better fit.

Developer

- Motivated by basically one drive, the **Dominance** need. "Full steam ahead!"
- Developers are extremely self-reliant and independent in thought and action. They may lack empathy and seem uncaring.

- *Would strengthen relationship with more:* patience; empathy; participation and collaboration with partner.

Results-Oriented

- Motivated by a **Dominance** need and a lesser **influence** need. "It's only the results that count."
- Results-oriented persons are impatient and fault-finding with those who are not quick in thought and action.
- *Would strengthen relationship with more:* genuine concern for their partner, patience and humility.

Inspirational

- Motivated by equally strong **Dominance** and **influence** drives. "I'm always here to help you!"
- Inspirational persons can be charming and persuasive. They are astute in manipulating another person's existing motives and directing the resulting behavior toward a predetermined end.
- *Would strengthen relationship with more:* genuine sensitivity and willingness to help partner succeed in his or her own personal development.

Creative

- Motivated by a strong **Dominance** need and relatively equal **Conscientiousness** need. "Tell me your ideas; then I'll tell you mine."
- Creative persons want freedom to explore. They can make decisions quickly but may be extremely cautious in making the bigger decisions.
- *Would strengthen relationship with more:* warmth; using more tact when communicating with partner.

The "i" Type Personalities

These are the enthusiastic and talkative types. They are **inspirational** and **influencing**. They can use their charm to influence others, and they like to be recognized. They have the ability to make everything sound great. Because they are great talkers, they are good at influencing others to their point of view.

If this snapshot description fits you or your partner's style, review the following four profile patterns listed below and see if you can find an even better fit.

Promoter

- Motivated by the single **influence** drive. "Hey! Isn't this fantastic?"
- Promoters are good at promoting their own ideas and creating enthusiasm in others.
- *Would strengthen relationship with more:* emotional control and follow-through on promises to partner.

Persuader

- Motivated by the **influence** drive and a lesser drive for **Dominance.** "I'm going to work with you to make sure you get what you want."
- Persuaders have the ability to bring people to their point of view. They also tend to overestimate their ability to change the behavior of others.
- *Would strengthen relationship with more:* listening to partner's point of view.

Counselor

- Motivated primarily by an **influence** drive and a lesser drive for **Steadiness**. "Everything's going to be just fine; I'm with you all the way."

- Counselors are good listeners and refrain from imposing their ideas on others. They often take criticism as a personal affront.
- *Would strengthen relationship with more:* initiative and expressing concerns more readily to partner.

Appraiser

- Motivated by primary **influence** drive and relatively equal **Conscientiousness** drive. "If we work together and follow the plan, we can make it happen."
- Appraisers tend to be skilled in helping others to visualize the steps necessary to accomplish desired results. Can become restless and critical when pressured.
- *Would strengthen relationship with more:* patience and less verbal criticism of their partner.

The "S" Type Personalities

These are the reserved, low-key and easy-going types. They are **steady** and **people-oriented**. They find it easy to get along with different types of people. They like to please people but prefer to go unnoticed. They are patient and loyal. Security is very important to them.

If this snapshot description fits you or your partner's style, review the following four profile patterns listed below and see if you can find an even better fit.

Specialist

- Motivated by basically one strong drive for **Steadiness.** "Well, we got it done on time."
- Specialists are considerate, patient, and always willing to help those they consider friends. They are slow to adapt to change.
- *Would strengthen relationship with more:* sharing of their ideas and being more assertive when communicating with partner.

Agent

- Motivated by a strong **Steadiness** drive and a lesser **influence** drive. "Just tell me what you would like me to do."
- Agents make people feel wanted and needed because of their responsiveness to the needs of others. They fear conflict.
- *Would strengthen relationship with more:* self-awareness of who they are and what they can do, and firmness and self-assertion with partner.

Achiever

- Motivated by a strong **Steadiness** drive and a lesser **Dominance** drive. "It's my idea. I want the credit and I'll take the blame."
- Achievers would rather do the task themselves so they can be sure it is done right. They sometimes get too absorbed in what they are doing.
- *Would strengthen relationship with more:* willingness to compromise and reduction of either/or thinking.

Investigator

- Motivated by a strong **Steadiness** drive, a secondary **Conscientiousness** drive and a third, lesser, **Dominance** drive. "I'm determined to find out what's causing this."
- Investigators are not especially interested in pleasing people. They can be perceived as coldly blunt and tactless.
- *Would strengthen relationship with more:* flexibility and more personal involvement with partner.

The "C" Type Personalities

These are the "task-oriented" types. They are **conscientious** and **calculating**. They dislike making mistakes and are driven by a need to

do things correctly. They are sensitive and attentive to people around them.

If this snapshot description fits you or your partner's style, review the following three profile patterns listed below and see if you can find an even better fit.

Objective Thinker

- Motivated by basically one strong drive for **Conscientiousness** (to own standards). "Just the facts, please."
- Objective thinkers emphasize the importance of drawing conclusions and basing actions on facts, seeking correctness and accuracy in everything they do. Under pressure they become worrisome.
- *Would strengthen relationship with more:* self-disclosure and sharing their ideas and opinions with partner.

Perfectionist

- Motivated by a strong drive for **Conscientiousness** and a relatively equal **Steadiness** drive. "Let's take time to do it right the first time."
- Perfectionists are systematic and precise thinkers who tend to follow procedure in both their personal and work lives. They fear antagonism and prefer stable conditions and predictability.
- *Would strengthen relationship with more:* belief in self as a worthwhile person and acceptance of sincere compliments from their partner.

Practitioner

- Motivated by a strong **Conscientiousness** drive, a secondary **influence** drive and a third, lesser, **Steadiness** drive. "Based on my experience, the most effective way to proceed would be…"
- Practitioners often project a relaxed, diplomatic and easygoing style. They give the impression of knowing something about

many things. They value self-discipline. Under pressure they become restrained.

- *Would strengthen relationship with more:* appreciation of their partner's contribution.

Some Examples of Classical Patterns

In order to further illustrate how some classical patterns interact and how these styles contribute to our successes, I will present some personal examples.

Both Susan and I have high behavioral tendencies. Susan is a high **"S"** or **Steadiness**, with a classical pattern of **Agent.** Empathetic and supportive, Agents seldom reject people. Too bad I didn't know that the first time I asked her to dance. I would not have experienced that approach-avoidance conflict, and been so nervous. Over the years she has made me feel wanted and needed, and as a partner is attentive to both our private and work relationship.

High "S"s are patient and loyal. For more than 25 years, Susan has stood by me, and was my strongest supporter when I decided to form my own company. In many ways we are a classic "opposites attract" couple, as I described earlier. Susan has a strong desire for steadiness and stability, while I like to experience change and variety. She brings a great balance to our relationship, and has often covered for my areas of weakness.

Agents are particularly good at doing for others what they find difficult to do for themselves. A perfect example of this trait is Susan's willingness to work hard at tracking and recording the financial aspects of our business, even though she hates spending time on her personal finances.

An Agent can make you feel comfortable and right at home. They believe in being polite. They value manners and are rarely pushy. They are the ultimate team players. This dimension of Susan's

behavior makes her a great asset during workshops. Her supportive approach helps the participants to feel at ease, facilitating their ability to work on their problems.

As an Agent, Susan fears conflict and is uncomfortable with aggression. Unfortunately this preference caused problems during the early years of our relationship when I would be very persistent about resolving our conflicts. To my great relief, she has adjusted her style. Susan is now less likely to avoid conflict, and is more self-assertive and willing to work until our disagreement is resolved.

I am a high **"i"** or **influence**, with a classical pattern of **Persuader.** Persuaders prefer to work with and through people. That's why I enlisted the help of a variety of people to help me with this book, rather than do it on my own. I continually asked for Susan's opinion and, even though I found it difficult at times to accept her criticism, I valued her insights and suggestions.

High "i"s are fast-paced as well as enthusiastic. For the past 14 years, whenever someone asks me how I am, I always respond with "Sensational!" I enjoy making a favorable impression, creating a motivational environment, and generating enthusiasm. High "i"s are good in one-on-one situations, but are even better in front of a group. I'll be the first to admit that I'm a bit of a ham when I get in front of a group. I will also jump at the first opportunity to appear before a crowd and speak, whether or not I'm prepared. I've often been accused of, and will admit to, "winging it."

Persuaders like to express their thoughts and feelings to others, and have the ability to bring people to their point of view. As I will share with you in Chapter 5: Conflict, I sometimes overused this persuasive tendency during the first years of my relationship with Susan. Persuaders are also particularly good at finding ways to interact positively in difficult situations. This ability has helped me to work well with couples who are experiencing distress and conflict.

A Persuader can inspire individuals as well as groups to want to improve themselves. They are also very good at making the learning

experience enjoyable. This strength has helped me tremendously as a couples coach and motivational speaker.

As a Persuader, I have a natural positive outlook and believe strongly in my ability to change the behavior of others—a belief I have had to temper, accepting the fact that I cannot change anybody unless they want to change. Unfortunately, this desire to change behavior did not always work when I tried too often to use it with my life partner. To Susan's great relief, I have adjusted my style to fit better with hers and to bring a better balance to our relationship.

What About Weaknesses?

Up until now, I have presented mostly the positive behaviors and preferences of the personality types. It is important to also point out that you will need to identify your weaknesses. It is generally accepted that weaknesses are simply strengths that have been taken to an extreme. This can often happen when you are under pressure and feeling anxious. Under these conditions you might use more of your strengths than are necessary, believing that more of a good thing will result in an even better performance. Unfortunately, when you overuse your strengths, they flip to the weakness side.

Some Examples:

People with high **"D"** or **Dominance**, are strong-willed, drivers, determined and good at directing and deciding. However, under pressure they may become autocratic. They may lose their temper and explode over what seems trivial. They also get over this anger and forget very quickly that it ever happened.

If you are a "**D**" person, you would benefit from pacing yourself and knowing when and how to relax.

People with high **"i"** or **influence**, are very friendly, compassionate, enthusiastic, and good at promoting and persuading. Under

pressure they may oversell and manipulate. Also, since they are "people-people" and want to be liked, they often struggle over disappointing anyone.

If you are an "**i**" person, you would benefit from understanding how and when to be more firm and direct in dealing with less favorable situations.

People with high **"S"** or **Steadiness**, are very patient, loyal and predictable. They are steady and agreeable. Under pressure they may give in despite their needs. They may also become very uncomfortable with new situations and environments.

If you are an "**S**" person, you would benefit from learning how to better handle the reality of unexpected and ongoing change.

People with high **"C"** or **Conscientiousness**, are accurate and systematic. They love details and are very analytical, capable of taking a situation and breaking it down to each individual component. Under pressure they may become perfectionistic and suffer from "analysis-paralysis," the fear of making a decision because they believe they don't have all the details.

If you are a "**C**" person, you would benefit from learning to develop a greater tolerance for conflict and human imperfection, including realistic approaches to preventing and minimizing both.

The Comfort Zone

As you can see from the above examples, whenever you are out of your "comfort zone" you run the danger of flipping to your weakness side. You could begin to overuse your strengths and apply too much of a good thing to the situation. The answer lies in accepting yourself as you are, and being in harmony with your internal feelings and preferences. When you stay focused on balancing your strengths according to what the situation demands, you will regain your confidence and feel in control.

When you are being yourself, you will experience a flow of behavior that seems to happen without conscious thought. In the sporting world, this experience is often referred to as "zoning" or "flow." It is as if you are watching yourself perform without trying. Your performance flows smoothly, without conscious effort. In your relationship, these moments can be described as those times when you are completely in touch with your partner. You experience each other as if nothing or no one else exists. You are in "the zone." You are experiencing joy.

How to Use the Results

The *DiSC® Profiles* present a plan to help you better understand yourself and your life partner. As you increase your understanding of your personality style and identify your typical behavioral patterns, you will be able to get the most out of your behavioral strengths, and appreciate the uniqueness of your partner. This new level of awareness will also help you to anticipate and minimize potential conflicts and to build a more secure bond.

You should also be aware that there is no "best" or "ideal" dimension of behavior or classical profile pattern. Many people incorrectly assume there must be one best way to connect with another person. In fact, there is no one classical profile pattern that is better than any other classical profile pattern. There is no best or worst, no good or bad profile. Therefore, satisfaction in your relationship is not connected to having a certain behavioral pattern. Satisfaction comes from knowing yourself, understanding your partner and adapting to the needs of the situation.

A Word of Caution

These awareness tools are not intended to encourage you to change

your or your partner's behavior. Instead, they are simply designed to help you identify strengths and possible limitations. Pressure for radical change would suggest that your or your partner's dimension of behavior or classical profile pattern is inadequate. The focus is on a willingness to become aware of and accept your behavioral pattern, and to develop skills to make yourself and your relationship more joyful.

It is also important to realize that even though the *DiSC® Profile Tools* are designed to give you another piece of the puzzle, they are not capable of giving you the whole picture. Granted, our lives would be simpler if someone's behavior could be totally described by one "most" and one "least" response. However, people are much more complex than that!

Don't lose sight of the fact that you and your partner are unique human beings who are constantly developing and changing.

Completing the *DiSC*®

If you would like to complete one of the *DiSC® Dimensions of Behavior* instruments, I suggest that you contact inscape publishing, formerly Carlson Learning Company, at 800-777-9897. They will be able to put you in touch with your local qualified inscape publishing distributor. These instruments are also available by contacting me directly by e-mail at: luke@thecouplescoach.com or check out my Web site: www.thecouplescoach.com for further information and assistance.

Reflect

The most satisfied partners are those who know themselves, recognize the demands of the situation and adapt strategies to meet those needs. Reflect on your uniqueness. Are you aware of your and your partner's strengths? Think about your unique strengths and how you can use them to keep your relationship healthy.

What do you need to do to develop your strengths and manage your weaknesses? Are you taking responsibility for your own growth and change, without attempting to change your partner? Jot down a few notes about what you *can* do, and what you want to accomplish.

Me

____

____

____

____

____

____

____

____

My Partner

____

____

____

____

____

____

____

____

A Beautiful Balance

Sometimes you change, and sometimes I change, and sometimes we both change. It is all a beautiful balance. It is a loving relationship where two people understand and accept each other's uniqueness.

Make a commitment to continue to grow, develop and change. List what strengths you will develop and weaknesses you will manage in the space below. Since you are in a loving partnership, discuss your choices with your partner. Choose what you consider to be the most important change you need to implement for a healthy relationship. Transfer this choice to your self-contract at the end of this book.

Me

My Partner

Communication

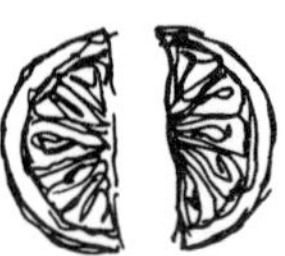

The gift of active listening is priceless because so few of us know how to give it.

The Need

"It feels so great when I'm understood."

One of our strongest desires is to be understood. To have another person, especially one we love, understand what we think, feel, value, love, hate, fear, believe in and are committed to, can be one of life's greatest pleasures. That is why I believe that effective interpersonal communication is such an important part of a healthy relationship.

We know the way we communicate not only plays a vital role in maintaining a healthy relationship, it also plays a very important role in our physical well-being. Just like the need for physical touch, the psychological need to be understood is important for our survival. Research has shown that poor adult interpersonal relationships can contribute to hypertension and coronary disease.

We also know that our relationship will suffer when we have trouble communicating effectively with our partner. In fact, the way we communicate is one of the chief causes of problems in our intimate relationship. It actually determines the kind of relationship we have, and whether or not our basic needs will be met. One of the basic needs that can be met through effective communication is our need to reduce uncertainty. We communicate to create a shared understanding of what is most important to us. As we learn more about our partner, and as they learn more about us, we are both better able to predict each other's behavior. This helps the world become a stable place, safer and more certain.

Interpersonal communication is also necessary to satisfy our needs for recognition and affection. The way our intimate partner communicates with us lets us determine how we are accepted, appreciated and loved. It was probably this kind of intimate communication that brought you together as partners. In fact, think back to that time when you first met, and you talked with your partner about something that was really important to you. Remember how you were listened to, and how you could tell that you were being understood? Your partner focused on everything you said. They hung on your every word. You saw they were really interested. How did you feel? I'll bet it felt great.

Now think back. When was the last time you experienced that kind of communication? Unfortunately, as I hear from many couples, those moments are rare. They often reminisce about the early days and say that they used to communicate like that when they first met. They long to recapture those moments.

That Special Closeness

The failure to recapture those intimate moments can lead to serious problems in a relationship. Some partners even stray and seek out

another person so that they might again experience that special closeness. That is what happened in the case of Mark and Dianna.

Mark and Dianna had been married for six years when Mark had an extramarital affair. After four months of "sneaking around," he admitted the affair to Dianna. During counseling, Mark described the frustration he often felt when he wanted to sit and talk with Dianna. He talked about how hard it was, especially in the evening: "There were nights when I felt like pounding my pillow. I would start to talk about something, and all I'd get back was silence. That's why it was such a great feeling when I met someone who not only listened, but also shared her feelings with me."

During a session I had alone with Mark, I asked him to tell me how the affair had begun. Mark explained that it had started while he was taking pictures at a wedding. He had been busy arranging members of the wedding party for some pictures, when he took notice of one of the bridesmaids. He recalls that what attracted her to him was how friendly and talkative she was. "I think I was more attracted to her personality than her looks. She was pretty, but I was just drawn to her openness. We started seeing each other about a week later, after I made some excuse about showing her some proofs of the wedding. You know, we didn't have sex until weeks later." Mark agreed to end the affair.

I should mention here that if I discover that one or both partners are having an affair outside of their relationship, I insist they end it before we can proceed with couple's counseling. That is why I suggest an individual meeting to see if there are any threats to the primary relationship. I will not agree to work with a couple unless they are both dedicated to making their relationship work.

I must admit that I believed Mark when he said, "It wasn't about sex. I just wanted to feel close to someone, to be accepted, to be understood. It's been a long time since I felt that at home. I'd give anything to have that again."

These kinds of experiences are not unique. The need to be under-

stood is extremely powerful. I do not deny that a healthy sexual relationship is also important for most couples. However, sex without closeness and understanding, is just sex. I believe that if an intimate partner has a good sexual relationship, combined with understanding and acceptance, he or she will never stray. I also believe that if a person has this kind of close and loving relationship, yet, in a moment of stupidity or weakness, have an illicit sexual encounter, they will do whatever it takes to heal the wounds caused by their lack of common sense.

Mark and Dianna were eventually able to heal the wounds, after some very hard and painful work by both of them. Dianna was able to share her fears with Mark, while he learned to support and encourage her. It was not that Dianna was unwilling to share her thoughts and feelings with Mark, it was her fear of rejection—a fear she had brought to their relationship from a previous and failed marriage. With time they both learned to experience the joy of understanding and being understood.

Effective interpersonal communication plays a vital role in maintaining a healthy relationship. Unfortunately, many couples assume that communication is easy and just comes naturally. They further assume that the way *they* communicate is the best and only way. The truth is that effective interpersonal communication does not come naturally, and there are many different styles…just recall the various personality types in Chapter 2: Change.

You can learn to communicate well enough to satisfy your basic needs, and to create a better relationship. You just need to work at it and agree as a couple that this effort is worthwhile and necessary. My hope is that you accept that the effectiveness of your communication skills will determine the health of your relationship.

Your ability to share and adapt to each other's needs will provide a secure base that can survive turbulent and stressful times. By sharing your inner thoughts and feelings with each other, you show how you genuinely care for each other. Through effective communication

you will learn how you are accepted, appreciated and loved by your intimate partner.

The more you feel that you understand your partner and are understood in return, the closer you will feel to one another.

Before I present some tips to improve your communication skills, I will share some personal experiences.

Back in 1996, I was participating in a workshop on treating couples. I was there to learn increased skills in providing couples with the tools to improve their relationships. At the very beginning of the workshop, one of the leaders asked us, "How many of you have learned some type of interpersonal communication theory to use when working with couples?" As I looked around, almost everyone, including myself, had raised a hand. Next she asked, "How many of you use it, and find it effective when working with couples?" Again, most of us raised our hand. Her third question was, "How many of you use it effectively when you are angry with your intimate partner?" Nobody raised a hand.

Now please don't assume that I'm suggesting that learning better communication skills is a useless exercise. I am suggesting that one the of rules of effective interpersonal communication is: **Don't try to communicate when you're angry!**

Let me illustrate:

One of Susan's favorite places to eat is a little restaurant that serves incredible pizza. It's quaint and comfortable, and at certain times it's not too busy. One day Susan was sharing with me that she'd had a particularly stressful day, so I suggested we go to this pizzaria and relax.

Now, something you need to know about Susan is that she was raised with a strong value for good manners. Behaving properly in public is important to her. Accordingly, I was on my best behavior.

So here I was relaxing with my best buddy. I was looking at her and thinking, *Here I am, about to have some great food, in the company of a woman who, after 25 years, still takes my breath away.* Life was very good.

Then the pizza arrived. In my eagerness to be a good host I quickly picked up the pizza cutter and removed a slice for Susan. Up to now everything was proceeding as it should. Then it happened. As I tried to transfer this rather juicy morsel to her plate, it somehow slipped off the utensil and fell, upside down, not quite making it to its destination. To make matters worse, I grabbed for it with my hands, turned it around, and tossed it onto her plate.

You guessed it. The look I got was not one that made me feel warm inside. I tried to explain how it happened, but she was not happy. I became aware of being upset, feeling hurt and getting angry. After all, it wasn't my fault the stupid thing slid off. That's when I also heard a little voice go off in my head, *Luke you know how to communicate, you teach other people how to do this, get it together and practice what you preach!* Now I'm thinking, *Just great! That's all I need right now. Criticism from her, and some more from me!*

The next words that came out of my mouth were not apologetic or kind, but defensive and aggressive. Thankfully, that voice in my head became less and less critical, and kept making suggestions. It reminded me that I was the one who had invited her out to make her day better. I guess my communication skills were working, internally at least.

Eventually I calmed down and apologized. I told Susan that I had wanted to please her and that embarrassing her was not part of the plan. I admitted that I had also felt uncomfortable, and that I had tried to cover it up by pretending it was no big deal. Happily she accepted my apology. You might say we kissed and made up, and the rest of the evening was "sensational"!

What Happens When We're Angry?

What often happens when we're angry is that we get defensive. And, as I just illustrated with my personal example, you stop communicating effectively. As Virginia Satir pointed out, in her book *Peoplemaking,* when we feel embarrassed, anxious, threatened and helpless, we go "on the defensive." We defend against feeling worthless. In fact, when we feel a lack of confidence or low self-esteem, we usually begin to communicate in ineffective ways. Our main concern is to defend ourselves.

When we feel good about ourselves, and we don't feel stressed or threatened, we will communicate with our partner in our normal manner. However, when we get defensive, our communication style can change dramatically.

Communicating in a defensive way will not bring you closer to understanding, but instead causes misunderstanding and more of a rift.

Equal Partnership

So far in this book, I have been writing about accepting each other, understanding one another, and creating a more loving relationship as equal partners. Communicating more effectively with each other is yet another way to achieve this kind of relationship. That means you treat each other as equals. You refrain from attacking, or criticizing, or acting superior or even defenseless. That means you stop yourself from saying statements like: "You're so inconsiderate." "You're always making me late." "You should be better at managing the finances." "Why do you always spoil things when we're ready to have a nice evening?"

You take responsibility for the way you communicate, and accept that when you threaten your partner's self-esteem you will likely get back an inappropriate response. You also take responsibility for building up your own self-confidence so that you will feel less defensive and not find yourself responding in an aggressive, boring, apologetic or irrelevant way. **Communicating in this caring and equal manner will result in a more satisfying relationship.**

Talk So Your Partner Will Listen

A number of books have been written on the subject of how women and men communicate. Some of these books seem to put both men and women into neat little boxes and state things like: "All men prefer brief exchanges, they don't like to talk things out." "Women get very emotional, and they like to talk a lot." I agree that these statements may be accurate for a great number of women and men. However, I do get concerned when I see a person adapt their communication style without checking to see if their partner fits the category.

I believe that a model is useful to explore our unique styles and to increase our awareness. I also believe that all of us have the capacity to change and adapt our communication style, and that at times we can be unpredictable and pleasantly surprising.

What I suggest is that you get to know your partner. Ask them if they have a preference. You may hear: "I'd like it if you got to the point more quickly," or "I find it easier to listen when you're not so emotional." You might find it interesting to know that a woman expressed both of these statements.

There are some general guidelines that are useful to remember when you want to express a concern to your partner. They are:

1. Treat your partner with respect.
2. Pick a time and a place that is comfortable for both of you.
3. Start off gently. Your opening statement will set the tone for what follows.

4. Be descriptive rather than evaluative. Focus on your partner's behavior and simply describe it—without *evaluating* statements like: "You're really inconsiderate."
5. Use "I" statements and take ownership of your feelings: "I felt embarrassed when you said that in front of my friends," rather than "You embarrassed me in front of my friends."
6. Express your feelings without judging your partner: "I'm worried about our finances," rather than "I'm worried because you are so careless with our money."
7. Phrase your concern in "more or less" rather than "always or never" terminology: "You forgot to take the dog for a walk *twice* this week," rather than "You *always* forget to take the dog for a walk."
8. Talk about your concern sooner rather than later: "When I came home tonight..." rather than "Remember last month...?"
9. Express your concerns only if it will be helpful for your relationship, not just to "get it off your chest."
10. Limit your talk to the amount of time and number of issues that are comfortable to absorb.
11. Explore alternatives that work for both of you, rather than presenting right and wrong answers. Make it a win-win situation.
12. Ask questions that relate to what, how, when or where. Asking "why" may lead to playing "amateur psychologist."

How Important Is Listening?

The answer is, "very important." It is one of the most important communication skills to learn and do well. It is also the one communication skill I hear most couples complain about. Concerns such as, "He never listens to me," or "She tunes me out whenever I start talking," are often expressed. Individual partners are starving to be heard. Some partners even describe the act of not being listened to, as being painful. They say, "It hurts when I'm not being listened to."

The problem is not always an uncaring partner. Sometimes a person may believe they are a good listener when in fact they are not. They do not realize that listening is hard work. They treat listening as if it was a spectator sport. What that means is that they sit back passively and hear what their partner is saying but they are not actively involved in the listening process. Effective listening means being involved. It is active, not passive. It also does not mean simply hearing. Some people protest, "I'm a good listener; I can even repeat everything she said." The problem is that these people make the incorrect assumption that the mere act of allowing their partner to talk is equal to listening. They take listening skills for granted and often assume they are better at listening than they really are. They also assume that simply hearing and remembering means understanding.

Employers were among the first people to recognize the importance of good listening skills. They read the studies that show that employees are required to spend most of their time listening. Even in today's e-mail world, voice mail and face-to-face communication demands a great deal of our attention and energy. These employers realized that a great percentage of an employee's salary was paid to them for the skill of listening. They were also aware that employees listened at an efficiency rating of only 25 percent (see page 88: *Is It So Hard for You to Listen?*). That meant a lot of wasted money due to misunderstood instructions.

Even in the world of sales, where traditionally people were taught to speak more effectively and go for the close, they learned that salespeople who listened more than they talked, made more sales. So now the emphasis is on letting the customer talk while you listen. The focus has become: "First find out what they want, understand their needs and build a relationship." The same is true in the area of customer care. No wonder there has been a growing trend in the business community of sending employees to listening skills courses.

The good news is that a lot more people have learned to improve their listening skills. The bad news is that when these very same skilled listeners come home, they are often too tired to listen any more. The conscious effort required, to concentrate on the words and to listen for the complete message their partner is sending, can be too much. They revert back to their poor listening habits and become "spectator" listeners.

Is It So Hard for You to Listen?

Have you ever been asked this question in an accusatory tone? If you have, I suggest you answer, "Yes it is!" As a matter of fact it is very hard. When it comes to communication skills, listening is the hardest one of all. I have been teaching interpersonal communication skills for over 25 years, and even though I pride myself on my ability in this area, there is still much room for improvement.

So why is it so hard to listen effectively? Well, it has actually been tested. Dr. Ralph G. Nichols headed a national committee in the US devoted to research in effective listening and found that we listen at a proficiency rating of only 25 percent. These tests of comprehension show that without training we are not very good at listening. I suppose these results should not surprise us simply because most of us have never received any training on how to listen. Think back to your school days and I'm sure you can remember lessons on reading and writing. You may even remember some attempts at teaching you to speak properly. However, I don't recall ever taking a class in listening. It seems that the assumption was made that listening simply requires paying attention, and hearing what was said. Many couples have manifested a similar assumption.

Listening is a demanding process and requires extra energy. It demands concentration and the tuning out of distractions. It is an active process. It is also the one form of communication that we are

required to use most often. You may be surprised to know that a recent survey, described in the book *Interplay: The Process of Interpersonal Communication* by Ronald Adler, shows that during the day we spend on average 53 percent of our time listening. The survey breaks our communication activity down as follows: writing, 14 percent; speaking, 16 percent; reading, 17 percent; face-to-face listening, 21 percent; and mass listening, 32 percent. So you see, not only does listening require more energy than any other form of communication, it also demands the lion's share of our time.

Besides not being trained in such a demanding skill, another major problem is our limited attention span. We live in a talk-oriented society. We get inundated with all kinds of communication babble that is sometimes difficult to escape. Have you ever noticed how the volume of a television commercial seems louder than the program you're watching? Is it any wonder we learn to tune out in the midst of all that noise?

We are also used to being entertained. How often have you found it difficult to listen to a person who talked in a monotone manner, or whose voice did not sound pleasant? Maybe you found the subject matter boring so you escaped and let your mind wander to more pleasant thoughts. Perhaps you will admit that unless the speaker is interesting and can excite you with their style or topic, you just won't listen.

There is another, perhaps even more dangerous, problem. It is called "giving advice." Well-meaning or not, we often find ourselves giving advice to people who didn't even ask for it. Our society seems to value problem solving and solution finding. So we rush in as soon as we can think up the answer. Now I'm not saying that solving a person's problem is wrong or not valuable. You may find, however, that it is more valuable to allow others the benefit of making their own decisions. This is especially true in your loving relationship. You may recall what I wrote about my own tendency to advise Susan on what kind of books she should read during the beginning

years of our relationship. Believe me, even if your partner asks for advice, active listening may be the only thing that is required. In fact, any attempt at giving advice without first listening to the full story and understanding your partner's concern, may just create more problems.

Take, for example, a situation where your partner comes home from a rough day at work and tells you: "My job is the pits. My stupid boss was being a ________ again. I should just up and quit." What do you do? Is it best to tell them to quit? To stop putting up with all that crap? Would it be safer to say, "I think you should stick with it. It will get better. You'll see." Or should you just listen, and let your partner vent? As you will discover later in this chapter, the best course of action may be to listen first and understand before you choose your response.

Here are some other reasons why it is so hard to improve your listening skills, along with some suggestions:

1. **I'm not interested.** Do you ever find yourself thinking, "This stuff he's talking about is really boring," or "I hope she's finished talking soon so I can get back to what I was doing." Well if you do, you might as well accept that you are not listening. To improve your skill, simply search for something of interest to you. Develop a frame of mind that is curious and know that no matter what your partner is talking about, there is always something worth understanding.
2. **I get tired when I'm listening.** We all do, as a matter of fact. Listening takes energy. More energy than talking. So do yourself a favor and exercise your mind. Develop your capacity to listen. When you work at getting yourself in physical shape, you increase the level of difficulty, and eventually what used to be hard for you becomes easier. Improving your capacity to listen works in the same way. Every time you raise the bar, and stick with it, you will improve. You will have more energy to listen.

3. **I get distracted.** Do you find yourself being easily distracted by the TV, radio, or some other sound? If that's the case, find a quiet place, or simply turn off the distraction so you can focus on your partner.
4. **I can't get a word in.** How often do you jump in and offer your opinion, or start to talk about your agenda? If the answer is even, "just sometimes," then you're not listening. You cannot listen if you are talking. You are also not listening while you are preparing your response. So this one is easy: Stop talking!
5. **I find myself thinking about other things.** Now this one is a major problem. Did you know that we are not really designed to be good listeners? I say this because most people talk at a speed of about 125 words per minute. Yet, we think at a much faster rate. Research shows that we can think at a rate four times faster than a person can speak. That means your mind can be thinking of about four words while your partner has only been able to say just one. The answer is, of course, concentration. Focus on what your partner is saying. Listen between the lines. Pay attention to the whole message including the non-verbal communication.

Difficult as it is, listening skills can be improved. Better listening between partners will lead to a greater closeness and a healthier relationship.

You're Not Listening!

How often have you made the above statement to your partner, or they have said it to you? If your answer is "too often," then please join the rest of us. This problem usually happens when we are not paying as much attention to our listening habits as we are to other things. We sometimes engage in listening habits that annoy and

sometimes anger our partner. Now in case you are saying, "I never do that!" see if you recognize any of the following habits:

My partner…

(a) interrupts me when I talk;
(b) never sits still;
(c) finishes my sentences for me;
(d) looks at clock while I'm talking;
(e) looks out the window;
(f) glances at the television or computer screen;
(g) never looks at me while I'm talking;
(h) looks me in the eye but never smiles;
(i) smiles even when I'm talking about a serious problem;
(j) doodles and draws pictures while I'm talking;
(k) acts like listening to me is doing me a favor;
(l) answers a question with another question;
(m) shows no expression to let me know if I'm being understood;
(n) frequently asks me to "get to the point;"
(o) tries to get me off topic with irrelevant questions and comments.

____

____

____

____

Understanding and Being Understood

During my communication classes and workshops, I always ask the participants to give me their definition of "effective interpersonal communication." I also ask them to remember that communication is a two-way process and that the definition should be made up of no more than ten words. In my opinion, the best definition that has

ever been presented is: *Understanding and being understood.* It is simple, yet says it all.

Simple or not, the experience of being understood and understanding our partner is a powerful one. Not only does this experience open us up to personal healing and growth, it also greatly improves the quality of our relationship. Through better communication, our loving relationship will become stronger and we will feel more secure. **Love grows when we are understood and accepted.**

In order for this love and growth to happen, however, we must be willing to expose ourselves to our partner—to share our thoughts and feelings at a level we perhaps have never done before. Unfortunately, we are sometimes afraid to reveal our inner selves. We hide behind our intellect and only expose what we think is comfortable and safe. Perhaps we are unaware that our relationship can only be as good as the level of our communication, or that the level of our communication is revealing of the amount of trust and comfort that exists in our relationship.

Over the years I have developed a guide to determine at what level a couple may be in their communication. It is useful to find out where you are, so that you can decide whether or not there is room for improvement. See if you can identify the level at which you normally reveal yourself (your self-communication) and use to relate to your intimate partner. Then decide at which level you would like to be. A review of these levels should give you and your partner a good opportunity for discussion.

A reminder: This is an awareness opportunity, not a reason to label, attack or lay blame. It is only to be used to encourage growth and development.

Level 1: Superficial Conversation

This level represents the lowest level of self-communication. On this level you are only sharing yourself in a very superficial way. You

talk in clichés, like: "Hope you had a good day." "Things went OK at work today." "Looks like the weather is changing." You ask the kind of questions that don't tend to elicit a meaningful response: "How are you?" "How are things going?" "What have you been doing?" In fact, if your partner actually responded and told you how they really were, you would probably be surprised.

At this superficial level you say things you don't really mean, and you do not expect an honest response to your enquiries. Your partner will usually reply with a similar superficial comeback, like: "Hope you had a good day, too."

When you are communicating in this superficial way you are not sharing or exposing any part of yourself. Think of the word "**FINE**" as an acronym, meaning **F**eelings **I**nside **N**ot **E**xpressed.

This is really non-communication, because you remain isolated and alone.

Level 2: Just the Facts

From 1952 to 1970, there was a popular program on television called *Dragnet*. It was a detective series. What struck me at the time was that the head detective, Sergeant Joe Friday played by Jack Webb, when questioning witnesses, would interrupt them if they began to give too much information. He would cut in and say "Just the facts, ma'am." So you see, on this level, you begin to communicate a little less superficially; however, you expose almost nothing of yourself. You talk about what people said or did. You don't present any personal information about these facts. You simply report them.

Your conversations revolve around other's lives, and you keep your own experience hidden. You might talk about what people did at work, or discuss something you saw in the newspaper. You also do not expect your partner to share personal experiences with you.

Unfortunately, as long as you fail to share yourself, you will be unreachable, and you still remain alone.

Level 3: Just a Little Exposure

At this level you begin to communicate something about yourself. You show a willingness to reveal ideas, judgments and decisions. However, you remain guarded. It's like you are watching your partner to make sure that what you say will be accepted. If you sense any rejection you quickly retreat back to the previous level.

Your conversations revolve around topics that you suspect your partner would want to hear. You're simply trying to please.

You dream about someday having the courage to say what's really on your mind and in your heart.

You feel a little less lonely.

Level 4: From the Heart

Once you begin to reveal your ideas, judgments and decisions, you start to realize that there is more to communicating than just saying what's on your mind. If you want your partner to know who you really are, you must be able to share yourself on a feeling level. Say what's in your heart.

It is good to express what you think; however, revealing the feelings that lie beneath your ideas is better. Sharing your hopes, fears and uniquely personal emotions will bring you closer to being understood. I realize that sometimes we are afraid of how much power our feelings actually have, and the effect they can have on us and on our partner. We sometimes attempt to hide our feelings, particularly the negative feelings such as anger, resentment or disappointment.

It is not necessary to reveal everything you feel. In fact, it may be harmful to simply "dump" all your feelings on your partner. What

is important is that you share those feelings that are necessary for understanding, and only to the extent that is comfortable for you and your partner.

At this level you are connecting at a "heart level." You are willing to expose, and risk, your deeper self.

Friendship and love begin to grow as communication becomes honest and deeply revealing. You are no longer alone.

Level 5: Simply the Best

You have reached the highest level when what you say to each other is absolutely open and honest. You experience a complete and personal connection. You are no longer afraid to expose who you really are.

At this level you willingly share your fears and desires. You allow your emotions to rise to the surface, and you are "in touch with" your partner's emotions. I'm not suggesting that you surrender to your emotions. Instead you have achieved emotional maturity, and a healthy balance of senses, emotions, intellect and will. You are able to express and accept feelings of affection and tenderness.

I realize that to communicate at this level is not easy, and to expect to relate at this level all the time would be unrealistic. I don't believe that many, if any, of us have reached a level of security where we no longer fear rejection. However, I do believe that there is in each of us a deep and driving desire to be understood. Working with your loving partner to reach this level of peak communication is well worth the effort.

When you are able to understand, and be understood, not only are you are no longer alone, you are connected to your partner.

Put Yourself in My Place

Empathic listening is one of the best ways to truly understand your partner. It is also a very important skill that, when used effectively, will strengthen your relationship. When you practice empathy, your first goal is to understand your partner, to see and feel what your partner sees and feels. The meaning of the word "empathy" actually derived from two Greek words that mean "feeling (in)side." The most common saying used to describe it is "to walk a mile in their shoes." When we say we are empathizing with someone, we are *experiencing* the other person's perception. We are temporarily becoming them, and their experience becomes our own. **You might say that you are temporarily crawling inside your partner's skin and seeing the world through their eyes.**

On the cognitive level, empathy involves understanding your partner from their perspective or point of view. It does not mean that you must accept your partner's view. It simply means that you understand it. However, to fully understand your partner, cognition is not enough. Connecting only with your intellect, while not understanding the richness of your partner's feelings, is no better than if you were a computer. You may be able to remember the words but you will not understand their true meaning.

Empathic listening involves using all your senses and skills to understand your partner. You might be interested in knowing that in Chinese, the verb "to listen" is made up of the characters representing ears, eyes, undivided attention and heart.

Empathic listening is probably the most difficult form of interpersonal communication. As Stephen Covey writes in *The 7 Habits of Highly Effective People*, "Most people do not listen with the intent to understand; they listen with the intent to reply." We are just itching to get a word in ourselves. We get so caught up with our own agenda that we find it very difficult to suspend our judgments, and we fail to see things from the other's point of view. Sometimes, when we hear things

that go against our own belief systems, we may block out the message, or distort it to fit our reality. And of course there are those favorite "hot buttons" (a concept you can read more about in Chapter 5: Conflict) that trigger our emotions. A single word or phrase can stimulate a reaction in us that interferes with our ability to understand.

So if you really want to help, and be helped, the answer lies in staying focused on your partner and suspending your own judgment. Forget about having the right answer. You may not even understand the question. I can't tell you how often I have heard the complaint: "I don't listen any more because he/she is always nagging about the same thing." Usually in our relationships we talk a lot about "stuff." We talk about the kids, the job, money, the house. Yet, our concerns are rarely about this "stuff." Instead, we are truly concerned about our deep inner feelings. We may be afraid of rejection, or think that we don't have a right to ask, or we are just not confident and secure enough to risk exposing our inner desires. No matter what the fear, the result is that we end up talking about the same things over and over again, and the real issues never get resolved. No wonder I hear so many people talk about how lonely they feel.

So, you may ask, what's the answer? **The answer is, understanding each other on an emotional level.** This involves not just listening and hearing what is said, but being able to understand the underlying message, the real meaning behind the words. Empathic listening is an excellent way to find out what's buried beneath all that "stuff."

Remember the example I gave about your partner complaining about his or her job? Let's look at the case of Debbie and Steve and see if you recognize any of your own issues:

Steve expressed his frustration that, for weeks, Debbie had been coming home and "bitching about her job." "It doesn't matter what I say, she's never happy with my answer or suggestions. I even told her that she could quit. I said that I wish she would quit just so she would stop all that bitching."

Debbie responded with: "He doesn't understand me. He says he's supportive but all he does is tell me not to complain and to learn how to manage my new boss better. He's always reminding me that we need the money and that he doesn't like his job either but he does it anyway."

When they were able to get to the underlying emotional level, it became clearer that Debbie just wanted Steve to accept and understand that she felt scared about meeting the demands of her new boss. She felt overwhelmed with the pressure and the expectations at work, and she was looking to Steve for some nurturing and acceptance. I want to point out here that we sometimes look for this kind of support from our work environment. Unfortunately, that may be the wrong place to look. We may occasionally get some recognition, but to expect to be nurtured or cared for is often unrealistic. Debbie's inability to express her deeper underlying emotion left her frustrated and resentful.

Steve was also not able to express his needs. He assumed that he had to solve her problem. And since he didn't even know what the problem was, he felt continually frustrated. His need for acceptance revolved around doing the right thing. When confronted by Debbie about the pressure she felt to stay at this job, he was unable to tell her that she was more important to him than "some dumb job." He wanted her to be happy, so he continually tried to fix the problem—a problem he was unable to fix, not only because he didn't understand it, but also because he only looked at Debbie's problem from his own perspective.

What helped them both was learning to empathize. Let me illustrate how you can develop this skill:

1. Sit facing your partner. Pick a topic for discussion where you have felt stuck.
2. Debbie starts by expressing her concern: "I hate my job." Steve then paraphrases what he hears: "What I hear you saying is that

you hate your job." This may feel strange and phony at first. However, you are learning to simply *understand* without judging or forming your own interpretations.

3. Debbie responds to confirm that his response was accurate. If Steve had not been accurate, the process would be repeated until understanding is confirmed.
4. Debbie continues to explain her concerns while Steve paraphrases what he hears. Eventually Steve could express what he hears using his own words but still showing an accurate understanding of Debbie's concern.
5. As the comfort level increases, Steve can begin to reflect and question, and mirror both *thoughts* and *feelings*. "You feel scared because this guy is new and you don't know yet what he wants. How different is he from your last boss?"
6. As understanding increases, you discover the deeper levels that are not expressed. "Sounds like you really miss your last boss and the way he used to compliment you."

As Steve became more skilled at reflecting and feeding back accurately what Debbie was saying, he began to understand that she did not need his advice and only wanted his support. She was skilled at her job, and only needed some reassurance while she was adjusting to the changes. Debbie also realized that Steve wanted to help and would have supported her even if she had decided to quit.

This example illustrates that we can be very helpful if we just show an understanding of our partner's feelings and ideas. By reflecting back, it allows our partner to see the problem more clearly and allows them to create their own solution. By accepting their emotions, we are creating a level of comfort and security that leads to a greater closeness.

Empathy leads to understanding and being understood.

It has been said that total empathy is impossible. No person can ever understand another completely because of our unique differences and the limitation of our communication skills. Sometimes it can be hard for us to imagine how we would feel in a similar situation. The example I give most often is that, as a man, it is impossible for me to experience childbirth. However, the restriction of not having, or being able to experience, an event does not mean you cannot attempt to understand it. As partners, you can help each other understand.

When it comes to a loving relationship, the ability to get close to excellence is an indication of the success of two caring partners who are emotionally connected.

I See and I Understand

What you *do* can have more impact on your communication then what you *say*. According to Dr. Albert Mehrabian, a U.C.L.A. researcher in the field of nonverbal behavior, your communication effectiveness depends on the following:

- 7 percent on the words you say (the message itself);
- 38 percent on how you say those words (tone, variety, projection, resonance); and
- 55 percent on your body language (what your partner sees).

That means that a whopping 93 percent of communication has nothing to do with the actual words we use. I guess that old saying "a picture is worth a thousand words" has been proven by research. Workshop participants will often ask me if that means that what they say is not important. My tongue-in-cheek reply is usually, "Politicians have known about this for years. Forget content. As long as they look and sound good, people will vote for them."

To prove the importance of nonverbal and visual impressions, try a little experiment with your partner: Sit facing your partner, look them in the eye and say, "I love you." However, as you say the words, frown and shake your head from side to side as if you are signaling "no." If that doesn't confuse them, I don't know what will.

It seems that we place greater belief in what we see than what we hear or what is said. If you have had the experience of talking to a person who is not familiar with your language, you know that a lot can be interpreted from nonverbal messages. We often make assumptions about a person's friendliness and how approachable they are by the way they look. So remember, even though you're not saying anything you're still communicating. It is true when they say it's impossible *not* to communicate.

If you want to create an environment that will make good communication easier, I suggest you use the S.O.F.T.E.N. approach. This approach, using nonverbal cues, will contribute to making the discussions with your partner more satisfying, perhaps even enjoyable. It consists of the following six key behaviors:

Smile: As a first impression, an appropriate smile creates a pleasant tone. It lets your partner know that this is going to be a good discussion.

Open posture: Use your body language to show that you are willing to listen and that you are open to new ideas.

Forward Lean: A slight lean towards your partner gives the impression that you are interested and paying attention.

Touch: A hug, a kiss, a rub on the back, these caring gestures convey the message that you want to feel close and be in touch with your partner.

Eye contact: Face your partner and gently look them in the eye (not a staring contest). You are showing that you want to get the full message.

Nodding: The occasional nod gives your partner the message that you are listening and that you understand what is being said.

The fact that our visual presentation is of great importance does not mean we can forget about our vocal and verbal skills. It is still important that you make an effort to communicate with words that you want your partner to understand. Words are still the best way to communicate your thoughts and ideas, while nonverbal communication is one of the best ways to express your feelings and attitude. Unfortunately, some nonverbal behavior can be misunderstood.

My favorite example about ambiguity is a photo in the book *Interplay*. I asked the participants in a workshop to look at this photo and to give me their interpretation of what the couple is experiencing. What they saw was a couple clinging to each other with what looked like pained expressions on their faces. The man's eyes were squeezed shut, his brow was furrowed, and his mouth was slightly open and turned down at the sides as if he was in agony. The interpretation I got was that the man looked like he was suffering, was in pain and about ready to cry, and that the woman looked worried and afraid. Then I asked the group to read the caption, which said: "This couple has just learned that they won one million dollars in the New Jersey state lottery."

The most effective way to get your message across as clearly as possible is to combine the content of your message with a corresponding nonverbal message. This kind of communication is called *congruent sending*. When the content and the feeling you show to your partner are both the same, there is less of a chance of being misunderstood.

Just remember the power of your facial expressions, gestures, voice tone, or other nonverbal messages. Do not try to hide your

feelings, since a lack of visual cues will make interpretation more difficult. These signals represent a major resource in your ability to be understood. Combine these signals with the corresponding and appropriate words and you increase the power and effectiveness of your communications.

Congruent sending as a communication skill is very useful when you want to solve a problem or resolve a conflict.

By now you understand how difficult it can be to understand and be understood. I have described how active listening, nonverbal communication and congruent sending will greatly improve your chances of making this happen. Well let me tell you, I thought I knew all this stuff and considered myself a pretty good communicator during the first years of my relationship with Susan. It wasn't until one fateful day, on my way to a meeting, that I learned the truth about my abilities. I was driving, with Susan in the passenger seat, from Toronto to Ottawa. It had been a very pleasant drive while we shared our hopes and dreams, and talked about our future. The time seemed to have flown by as we entered the city limits more than four hours later.

That's when it started to happen. The meeting I was on my way to attend was important to me and I was feeling somewhat anxious to get there on time. I was unfamiliar with the city, so I asked Susan to take the map from the glove box and help me look for the location. Now before you start thinking, "That was your first mistake," I want to point out that the ability to interpret a map is not the exclusive domain of men. However, Susan does admit that she has difficulty making sense of "those darn maps"—something I was to become aware of in short order.

At that moment we were both experiencing some stress: Susan, because she was trying to find a street that she couldn't seem to locate on the map, and me, because I was starting to think I might be late. I was also in the middle of some heavy traffic and focused on

getting us there safely. As I tried to relax, I explained to her what to look for. I had been given some directions from the organizer of the meeting, so I described a short dead-end side street she should see before we got to the area.

As you may have guessed, we passed by this small street without a sound or any indication from Susan. She was just sitting there looking confused. Before I realized it, we were on a one-way street, stuck in traffic, with no hope of getting to my meeting on time. What ensued was a major fight, where both of us insisted we were right. I was adamant that I had been very clear with my instructions, while Susan was just as adamant, saying that my instructions were anything *but* clear.

It wasn't until a couple of years later that we learned why we sometimes think we are being clear and yet we still can't get the message across. I was taking a course in a communication technique called Neuro-Linguistic Programming (NLP). NLP was made famous by Grinder, Bandler, Cameron-Bandler and DeLozier. Since I will only present my personal understanding of the NLP techniques in very limited detail here, please visit your local bookstore or library if you want to find out more. There are many books available on this subject.

Two of the original books I read on the subject were Richard Bandler and John Grinder's book *Frogs into Princes*, and *Practical Magic*, by Steve Lankton. Basically they maintain that we human beings process information through three primary representational systems. They are: Visual (see), Auditory (hear) and Kinesthetic (feel). We use these three systems to understand our world, yet we have what is called a "lead" system through which we represent our experiences. This results in us having differences in what is called "digital presentation." The following is an example of how these presentations will differ according to a person's representational system:

Visual— "This looks really good and clear to me." "I see what you are saying."

Auditory—"Tell me in more detail what you are saying at this point in time." "This sounds really good to me."

Kinesthetic— "This feels really good to me." "I feel really good about what we are doing."

These differences are not usually a problem when we are relaxed. Although we may have a primary representational system, we usually understand a person who is using words typical to one of the other systems. The problems start when we are stressed and feeling anxious. When we start to experience pressure, we flip to our primary system and we have difficulty comprehending the others. It is as if the pressure we experience causes the computer in our brain to function with only one program and locks out the others. So now you know why two people who normally communicate quite well can suddenly have difficulty understanding one another.

In Susan's and my case, the problem started to happen when we both experienced stress. She started to feel stressed when she was asked to interpret the map, so she accessed her primary system (**auditory**). I was also feeling stressed because I was becoming concerned about not getting to the meeting, so I accessed my primary system (**visual**). Wouldn't you know it—another opposite! So here I was telling her to "see this," "look for that," and "you'll see it clearly marked." Susan, on the other hand, was confused because nothing "sounded right," nor was I giving her "the details or the right words."

This experience was one of the first to teach me the value of not trying to communicate when you are upset or stressed. I had been told that overstimulation and understimulation are the twin evils of inefficient listening. My problem doesn't seem to be understimulation. I just have to remind myself occasionally not to get so excited, and to take a deep breath.

The message is clear. The worst climate for effective interpersonal communication is one where both partners are feeling defensive,

angry or stressed. **The best climate is when both partners are concerned for each other, have high self-esteem and are relaxed.**

Twelve Steps to Better Communication

The following twelve steps are here for your review. Practicing the twelve steps will help you to achieve a closer relationship through better communication.

1. **Stop talking.** The first step to better communication is to keep quiet when your partner speaks.

2. **Put your partner at ease.** Use the S.O.F.T.E.N. approach. Help your partner to feel free to talk to you by creating a supportive communication climate.

3. **Empathize.** Put yourself in your partner's place. As I say in my visual way, "look through your partner's lens and see a different world."

4. **Behave as if you want to listen.** Stop what you're doing. Show that you are interested and that you want to understand.

5. **Remember your thinking speed.** Use your thinking speed wisely. Focus your attention on the words, ideas and feelings of your partner. Use the "extra" time to summarize what your partner has been saying.

6. **Get rid of distractions.** Choose a quiet place where you won't be disturbed. Don't fidget, play with your pen, doodle or shuffle papers. Tune in to your partner.

7. **Don't give up too soon.** Wait until your partner is finished and expresses a complete thought. "Patience is a virtue."

8. **Share the burden.** Good communication is a partnership. It is understanding and being understood. It demands energy and skills from both partners.

9. **Keep your cool.** Control your anger, When you are angry, you are focused on your own feelings and not your partner's.

10. **Ask questions.** Make sure you are understanding and receiving your partner's thoughts and feelings accurately. Get clarification by asking questions.

11. **Avoid being critical.** Criticism puts your partner on the defensive. Make it a win-win situation.

12. **Practice, practice and practice.** Make a commitment to improve your communication skills and keep practicing until it becomes a habit.

What Is Your Listening IQ? (Me)

The first step to improving any skill is to determine how skilled you are currently. You need to have a measurement of your ability before you can develop a strategy on how and what to improve. After reading each question, give yourself a score of one to five. When you finish, add up your score and review the results with your partner.

Never		Sometimes		Always
1	2	3	4	5

Do you like to listen to your partner talk?	_______
Do you listen until your partner has finished a complete thought?	_______
Do you look at your partner when listening?	_______
Are you able to ignore distractions?	_______
Do you stop what you're doing and concentrate fully on your partner?	_______
Are you able to put yourself in your partner's place?	_______
Do you ask questions to make sure you understand?	_______
Do you restate what was said to show your partner you got the meaning right?	_______
Do you encourage your partner to talk with an appropriate smile and nod?	_______
Do you hold off judging or criticizing your partner's ideas?	_______
Are you aware of certain words and phrases that trigger your emotions?	_______
Are you able to stay calm when your partner expresses a concern or problem?	_______

Total Points

Enter your total score here: _______

What's Your Listening IQ? (Partner)

After reading each question, give yourself a score of one to five. When you finish, add up your score and review the results with your partner.

Never		Sometimes		Always
1	2	3	4	5

Do you like to listen to your partner talk?	_______
Do you listen until your partner has finished a complete thought?	_______
Do you look at your partner when listening?	_______
Are you able to ignore distractions?	_______
Do you stop what you're doing and concentrate fully on your partner?	_______
Are you able to put yourself in your partner's place?	_______
Do you ask questions to make sure you understand?	_______
Do you restate what was said to show your partner you got the meaning right?	_______
Do you encourage your partner to talk with an appropriate smile and nod?	_______
Do you hold off judging or criticizing your partner's ideas?	_______
Are you aware of certain words and phrases that trigger your emotions?	_______
Are you able to stay calm when your partner expresses a concern or problem?	_______

Total Points

Enter your total score here: _______

Results

40 or above: Congratulations. You practice good listening skills. You are also contributing to a greater closeness and secure bond in your loving relationship. Continue to improve your skills and you will experience even fewer misunderstandings in your relationship. You will also improve your own emotional and physical health.

Below 40: Discuss with your partner what listening skills you do well. Find out what other listening skills would be appreciated, and determine which of these you would be willing to practice and improve. Every time you increase your listening skills you are contributing to a closer and more secure relationship. Listen to your partner, and you will be listened to.

Add your own: There may be other listening skills that you practice that are not described in the previous exercise. Discuss these with your partner and decide whether or not they qualify. Any listening skill that improves understanding will make your relationship better. Feel free to list these skills below. Score these skills and add the points to your results.

My own listening skill examples:

____

____

____

____

____

My partner's listening skill examples:

____

____

____

____

____

Reflect

Reflect on the effectiveness of your interpersonal communication. Can you remember times when you were listened to and understood? Do you feel that your partner understands you? Think about your relationship and how it is affected by your ability to communicate.

What do you need to do to become a better communicator? Are you taking responsibility for the level of communication in your relationship? Jot down a few notes about what you can do, and what you want.

Me

My Partner

A Beautiful Balance

Sometimes you talk and I understand, and sometimes I talk and you understand, and sometimes we both understand. It is all a beautiful balance. It is a loving relationship where two people, who have developed the ability to communicate, feel closer and understood.

Make a commitment to continue and improve your communication skills. List what you will do in the space below. However, since effective communication is a two-way process, *understanding and being understood*, work together as loving partners to develop your list. Choose what you consider to be the most important skill you need to improve for a healthy relationship. Transfer this choice to your self-contract at the end of this book.

Me

____

____

____

____

____

____

____

____

My Partner

____

____

____

____

____

____

____

Connection

And it is still true, no matter how old you are—when you go out into the world, it is best to hold hands and stick together.

Robert Fulghum
All I Really Need to Know I Learned in Kindergarten

The Attachment

"I want to feel safe and secure."

There are few things more frightening than the fear of losing the one you love. The feeling of insecurity, the fear of detachment or separation, is one of the strongest motivators for couples to work on their relationship. As a counselor I have seen the pain and suffering that can be caused by separation.

It is generally accepted that at birth we are totally dependent on others for our very survival. However, the importance of person-to-person contact doesn't end in the crib. The drive to experience comfort, care and protection remains with us for our entire lives. We will suffer both emotionally and physically if we are denied love and connection.

I am a firm believer that human beings are not designed to be alone. There is no such thing as total self-sufficiency. I'll even go so far as to say there is no such thing as being happy and alone. In fact, loneliness can kill. Human beings need relationships for their survival. All of us have emotional and physical needs that can only be provided through our connection with other people. It is our relationships with others that keep us alive. I realize that some people will say I'm suggesting we remain dependent on others for our entire lives, and that that is a bad thing. My answer is, "That's right, I am, and it is not an issue about whether it is good or bad; it is a necessity."

From the day we are born to the day we die, we are healthier when we are loved and securely connected to other caring people.

Love Makes You Live Longer

The fact that love makes you live longer has now been proven through actual research and long-term studies. Much of this information is available in a new book written by three psychiatrists. In *A General Theory of Love,* doctors Thomas Lewis, Fari Amini and Richard Lannon reveal seventy years of collective, clinical experience. What is most interesting is their revelation, backed by fresh scientific research, that reveals that prolonged separation affects our emotional well-being and also severely impacts our physical health. They state: "Cardiovascular function, hormone levels, and immune processes are disturbed in adults subjected to prolonged separation. And so medical illness or death often follows the end of a marriage or the loss of a spouse." The authors also report Dean Ornish's conclusion, from his review of the medical literature described in his

book *Love & Survival:* "Dozens of studies demonstrate that solitary people have a vastly increased rate of premature death from all causes—they are three to five *times* likelier to die early than people with ties to a caring spouse, family or community." If you truly want to understand the reason why it is so important to have a healthy relationship, I suggest you read this book.

The Science Of Love: Understanding Love and Its Effects on Mind and Body, written by Anthony Walsh, is another interesting book that focuses on current scientific research. Dr. Walsh investigated many different fields, including biology, genetics, brain physiology, psychology, and sociology. In it he states: "Love and hunger are drives, and drives are the physiological experiencing of a need to rectify some biological important deprivation....Love is a drive to unite so that the species may survive. The pains of hunger remind us that we must eat, the pains of romance that we must love."

If you are not yet convinced about the importance of connection and a healthy relationship, just have a look at the statistics that state that older men die soon after their partner dies, while women survive longer than men after losing their partner. The research suggests that the cause for the premature death of the men is that they seldom form secure and caring attachments with others, while women have traditionally depended on and gained strength from their connections and close relationships.

Oh, and by the way, if you are a younger man and you're thinking, "Luke's talking about older men, so I don't need to get too concerned yet," I suggest you think again. In this section I am truly concerned for the male of the species when it comes to connection. And in case you are wondering why, let me cite some important research specifically related to those of you who consider yourselves, "the strong and independent type." If that's you, you need to know about the medical hazards that result from the breakdown of a close relationship. In his excellent book *Bridges, Not Walls,* John Stewart states: "Divorced men (before age 70) die from heart disease, cancer, and strokes at double the rate of married men. Three times as many die from hypertension; 5 times as many commit suicide; 7 times as many die from cirrhosis of the liver; and 10 times as many die from tuberculosis."

All of this research confirms the healing power of love, connection and caring relationships. Perhaps now you can understand why I believe that: **Human beings need relationships. Our connection with other caring people keeps us alive.**

The Power of Interdependence

Earlier I stated that I did not believe in self-sufficiency. Well, I will admit that I did not always have this opinion. During my early years as a practicing psychotherapist, I used to conduct some singles' workshops that actually promoted independence. One of the statements I made back then went as follows: "Anyone who has developed insufficient strength to live alone, under-contributes to any relationship." The interpretation I gave was that we had to learn to be happy being alone so that we would not be so desperate for companionship. Fortunately, it did not take me too long to realize that the requirement for living a fulfilling single life is more about developing our capacity for self-love, self-confidence and self-worth. This inner strength will contribute to our ability to care for others as well as ourselves, a strength that enables us to develop and nurture caring relationships.

I came to understand that we should not isolate ourselves, but instead go out and seek out caring relationships. I accepted that people who have richer relationships enjoy better health. It was the work of John Bowlby that helped me to understand this concept. If you recall, I described some of his work in Chapter 1: Caring.

Dr. Bowlby's work on attachment and loss has demonstrated that the need to be in a secure relationship is adaptive and natural. Dr. Bowlby suggested that this type of contact is an instinctive survival

mechanism and plays a critical role in human development. Dependency is not a sign of immaturity or dysfunction; it is natural and part of the human condition. What this means is that the key to emotional and physical health is actually interdependence. The process involves our starting off as infants and being totally dependent on others. Then, on the road to maturity, we become independent, developing our capacity for self-love and self-reliance. Eventually we discover that we depend mutually on others for our well-being; we become interdependent.

Unfortunately, there are still many people in our North American culture who have a tendency to admire independence. Research now shows that that tendency may be the cause of our shorter lifespan and higher rate of heart disease than certain other cultures. In fact, just look at the Japanese culture. The Japanese have much in common with our culture. Many smoke cigarettes, have high blood pressure and experience stress. They live in overcrowded and polluted cities. All of these factors have been proven to contribute to disease and a shorter lifespan. Yet, amazingly, they live much longer than we do. They actually have one of the highest longevity ratings in the world. They also have one of the lowest occurrences of heart disease. So what's their secret? Well, scientists believe that it is the Japanese tradition of close personal ties to friends, family and community that is responsible for this phenomenon.

We Don't Survive in Isolation

Interestingly, the role of attachment and person-to-person contact can even be traced back to Roman days. The word "contact" is derived from the Latin *contactus* (touching), a word that is often used as a way of communicating, as in "Keep in touch!"

History has proven that human beings strive to be involved with others. We want to be part of a community. We don't survive in iso-

lation. In fact, you might be surprised to learn that in some primitive tribes, isolation is considered to be a form of capital punishment. I first learned about this cultural phenomenon some twenty years ago while I was showing the movie *You're Not Listening* to my interpersonal communications class. It featured a tribe living in Africa that practiced a unique form of justice. These aboriginal people sentence a person convicted of a capital offence to permanent isolation. The sentence is carried out in the following manner: The convicted person is declared to be a non-person. No one is allowed to communicate with them or to show any recognition of their existence. The result is usually that the convicted person will go out into the jungle and die.

Hopefully by now, I have presented enough evidence to convince you of the need for forming and maintaining close and healthy relationships. You may also understand my bias. I'll even say strong bias, in favor of a secure connection. I know that personally I have been convinced not only by the studies and research, but also by the clients I have seen who separated from their partners. On average, women adapted more quickly to not having an intimate partner because they had, or they re-established, caring relationships outside of their primary partnership. I should add that I am encouraged by the changes I'm seeing with some of my male clients. Many are recognizing that: **There is nothing like the healing power of a loving relationship.**

The problem today is that we are seldom connected to a large, caring and supportive community. Our society has changed tremendously in the last hundred years. How we live, where we live, and especially the structure of our families, have changed drastically. More often than not, we are separated from our extended families. We are a mobile society, and seldom stay in one place for long periods of time. The result is that the security we experience when we are part of a close-knit community and family disappears when we move to faraway places. We often settle into our new community, and even after years of living there, we only know our neighbors in a very superficial way. As Allan Fromme states in his book *The*

Ability to Love: "Our cities with their swollen populations and cliff dwelling high-rise buildings are breeding places for loneliness."

There is a rising trend of isolation and loneliness in our society. An increasing number of us are relying on our elaborate alarm systems for our safety and security, while our real protection, a caring and supportive community, is slowly disappearing. We are also placing an excessive amount of responsibility on our intimate relationship to be the sole supplier of our need for connection. What we used to get from a whole community, we now demand from a diminishing number of supportive people. Too often that number is one—our intimate partner. And that can become a very real problem. The pressure is often too much for one person to provide everything we need. When that happens, we start to experience loneliness and fear. Unfortunately, instead of maintaining our connection with our partner and working together to support each other, some of us react by closing ourselves off from the very person who can help us. We handle our fear by pretending we don't need this lifeline. We put on our armor, not even realizing that we are blocking out the very nurturing we require. Unknowingly, our fear can cause us to isolate ourselves even further. Statements like: "I don't need anybody; I do just fine on my own," just obstruct our view of reality. **As far as I know, solitary confinement has never been used as a reward**.

The solution lies in accepting that we need other people, and in working to build strong and healthy relationships. We also need to recognize that our primary relationship, the one we share with our loving partner, can be our best resource.

There Is a Problem with One "C"

The "C" in this case refers to "computer." I'm sure by now you have heard about or seen the reports on the newscasts that describe the growing problem with high users of the Internet. The reports I am referring to are claiming that millions of North Americans are addicted and hooked on the Internet. They also reveal that a great number of these people are suffering from loneliness and depression.

In my own practice I have noticed an increase in the number of people who are expressing their concern about the amount of time their partners spend on-line. They describe the negative impact it is having on their relationships. I find it especially sad when I hear a person talk about the hours they will spend communicating with a complete stranger and yet ignore their loving partner.

We used to ask our loving partners to turn off the TV. Now it seems the cry has become: "Turn off the computer." If you are asking 'how much time is too much?', my answer is: If you are showing signs of loneliness or depression, and you are not experiencing a strong connection with your partner, then you need to devote more time and energy to your relationship, and less to technology.

I am not suggesting that the problem is with the computer. The problem is with us, and how we use this technology. I have certainly met many couples and families that work together and see this computer age as an opportunity to share a common interest. They not only work together, they also play together. It is a healthy use of technology when it is used to bring people closer together. A word of caution: by being closer together, I mean "physically" together. It is a myth that technology can make us feel closer together if we are physically apart. Let's face facts: if the Internet made us "feel" closer, then these "net junkies" would not be experiencing loneliness and depression. They may be logging on and spending time in the "chat rooms," but they are lacking one extremely important ingredient. This ingredient is called "emotional connection."

This loneliness and technology is not a new phenomenon. Some people believed the advent of the phone would eliminate the loneliness of long distance relationships. If you think that is true, just ask the people who spend many days traveling and being away from caring relationships. They may be able to connect electronically, but

they still experience loneliness. When was the last time you spent some time at an airport and saw family members reunite after a long separation? The embraces, the kisses and the visible show of relief and joy can bring tears to your eyes, let alone theirs. You know exactly how they feel if you have been separated from a loved one for too long a time. No amount of letters, phone calls or "chatting on the Net" could relieve your longing.

I believe our culture is having a love affair with the wrong things. By that I mean that some people are trying to convince us that "things" can make us happy. The other day I saw a commercial on TV for a new truck. The words being touted to a susceptible audience were: "It's the best antidepressant you can buy without a prescription!" Well, if you believe that in the literal sense, you have a problem. True, an inanimate object can be used as a tool to provide you with some fun. For some people, and I'll count myself as one of them, cars can be that kind of tool. I'll also admit that I have experienced some fun driving on my own down some beautiful country roads. However, the feelings came from inside of me, not from the car. I've had similar feelings while biking and walking down the same roads.

The best antidepressant, as far as I'm concerned, is a loving relationship, where both partners are emotionally attached to each other. In fact, the important factor for the formation of a loving and secure relationship is connecting on an *emotional* level. True love can only grow out of an intimate and emotional connection with another person.

If you want to relieve your depression, make sure you are emotionally connected to your loving partner.

Emotional Connection

"It's the heart afraid of breaking that never learns to dance." This simple yet meaningful lyric, sung by Bette Midler in her song "The

Rose," speaks to many of us who are afraid to feel. Sometimes we are afraid of how much power our feelings actually have on ourselves and on others. We distrust how our feelings will be interpreted, and are afraid they will be misunderstood. So instead of opening up and sharing our innermost experiencs, we retreat and attempt to hide our feelings. This is especially true of negative feelings like anger, resentment or disappointment. The problem, of course, when we conceal our feelings, is that we will never be able to fully connect with another person. We will never experience the joy that comes from being accepted for who and what we are.

You will notice that throughout this book I stress the importance of feelings and emotions in building a healthy relationship. I also realize that many of us have not learned to express our emotions in a genuine way. What has made it difficult for us to express ourselves on a feeling level is the fact that intellectual, analytical and cognitive skills are highly valued in our society, especially in the business world. We learn, and are rewarded for, the appropriate use of logic. As a result, some of us have incorrectly assumed that our cognitive skills should override the expression of feelings. We talk like a computer, choosing our words carefully, and keeping our emotions repressed and securely locked inside.

Unfortunately, the lack of timely emotional expression interferes with our ability to achieve a human connection, the kind of connection that is necessary to understand and solve a "human" problem. As John Churton Collins once said: "Half our mistakes in life arise from feeling where we ought to think, and thinking where we ought to feel."

Fortunately, there is light at the end of the tunnel. Ever since Daniel Goleman's book *Emotional Intelligence* gained popularity, the "f" word, "feelings," has become more acceptable. Dr. Goleman is leading the charge and convincing the world of work that the most successful business people are those who have "emotional intelligence." He has demonstrated the "factors at work when people of

high IQ flounder and those of modest IQ do surprisingly well." It is encouraging that our society, which has traditionally placed a high value on thinking and independence, while the expression of emotions and dependence were seen as a lack of strength, is changing. Thank goodness Bowlby came along and showed us that dependency is not pathological. And now Goleman is leading the way in proving that being in touch with our emotions helps us to better understand and get along with others.

For a long time I have suggested that the number of his or her IQ cannot measure the level of a person's intelligence. My personal definition of an intelligent person is *someone who solves life's problems by using their intellectual and emotional talents to the best of their ability and uses that ability to make powerful connections with other people.* It is all about learning to express your emotions in an intelligent way and living a fulfilling life. I suppose that is why I agree wholeheartedly with Goleman's belief that really smart people are the ones who can connect emotionally with others and whose intimate relationships thrive and grow healthier.

I find it very encouraging to see more and more people in the business community accepting the need to establish an emotional bond. For example, I recently heard an executive recruiter talk about how he makes a decision concerning which candidate he will present to his corporate clients. To my pleasant surprise, he actually insisted that any person who was unable to establish this emotional connection would not move forward as a potential candidate. He would only consider them if the person was able to communicate at this high level. When asked how he could tell that this emotional connection existed, he replied that phrases such as "I trust him," "I feel good about him," "I like him," came to mind. He went on to describe that for him, and for a growing number of professional recruiters, it was becoming more of a feeling of knowing. "An experience that only exists as a result of combining what is in my head and in my gut."

Love and the Brain

Increasingly, people understand and accept the power of emotional connection. The current scientific research is becoming well-known. Both *The Science of Love* and *A General Theory of Love* present a fascinating description about the biological link in our brain. The studies presented in these books describe the important functions and connection between the various parts of the brain. The research they present shows how we are linked and how a close relationship can actually alter our physiology. Emotionally close people even change each other's hormones. Talk about connection! They even claim that the human brain is designed to be regulated by another human brain, and will not function properly in isolation.

All of this scientific research is finding answers to some age-old questions. Have you ever wondered why intimate partners have a habit of finishing each other's sentences? Well, now these researchers are proving that there exists a form of wireless communication. They are able to demonstrate why long-time partners will often start saying the same thing at the same time. What I found most interesting were the studies that show that lovers possess the ability to modulate each other's emotions. As stated in *The General Theory of Love*: "In a relationship, one mind revises another; one heart changes its partner.…Who we are and who we become depends, in part, on whom we love."

We now understand more fully why looking for a long-term, intimate and loving relationship is one of our strongest driving forces. It is part of our makeup. We want to be accepted, appreciated and loved by an intimate partner. And emotions play a major role. It is when we have formed an emotional bond with a loving, intimate partner that we feel most secure. Remember back to the day when you first realized you loved each other and wanted to become partners. You probably experienced a harmony, a sense of trust, optimism and mutual delight. You shared your feelings, and were open and

honest with each other. You made each other feel special. Probably without realizing it, you were experiencing emotional intimacy.

Emotional intimacy is the feeling of closeness and a deep emotional bond that is at the root of adult love.

The Fear of Feelings

I realize that it is not always easy for us to relate to each other on an emotional level. Fear of not being in control, or being embarrassed, keeps us from lowering our defenses. So we hide our emotions behind an objective, diagnostic or intellectual barrier so that we don't have to deal with our gut-level feelings. We are reluctant to expose ourselves. We hide. Whenever I say this, I am reminded of Hugh Prather's saying: "If a man takes off his sunglasses I can hear him better."

As I am writing this, I just experienced a flashback to the movie *Cool Hand Luke*. At the end of the movie, there is a scene where Paul Newman, playing Luke, is trying to make himself understood to a prison guard. The prison guard, who is wearing those mirror-style, reflective sunglasses, is not showing any willingness to understand. Luke, on the other hand, wants very much to make contact. You might say he is being rather emotional about it. At this point the guard lifts his rifle and shoots Luke. He then looks through his reflective glasses, not revealing any emotion, and makes this final statement, a statement indelibly imprinted on my brain: "What we have here, is a failure to communicate."

This failure to communicate happens too often in our lives. Don't let it happen in your loving relationship. If you want a lasting and loving relationship, don't settle for a superficial one. As revealed by John Gottman in his book *The Seven Principles for Making Marriage Work:* "What can make a marriage work is surprisingly simple. Happily married couples aren't smarter, richer, or more psychologically astute than others....They have what I call an emotionally intelligent marriage."

Whenever you can express yourself on a genuine feeling level you are being more open and honest. You increase your closeness. Your partner will experience you as being authentic, of being yourself, your total self and not just your intellect.

I accept the notion that intimate partners want to be emotionally attached in a secure bond. I also accept the fact that secure emotional attachment and personal independence can both be part of the same relationship. Being intimately connected to a loving partner will lead to self-acceptance and becoming more fully oneself. What all this means is that it is desirable to want a secure bond while still being your own person.

Have the courage and the strength to be open and honest with your partner. Accept and share your deepest feelings. Remember that your feelings are unique and reveal the inner you. As stated so insightfully by Hugh Prather in *Notes to Myself*: "I am beginning to think that there are no destructive feelings, only destructive acts, and that my actions become destructive only when I condemn and reject my feelings."

If you want your partner to know you in an intimate and real sense, be authentic and share your innermost feelings.

The Case of the Emotionless Man

Stephen had a doctorate degree in chemistry. He had written dozens of papers and several books on the subject. By society's standards he was a brilliant and gifted man. He had received many awards and was admired by his peers for his success. His marriage, however, was a complete and utter failure. Married to Anne for 23 years, Stephen had reluctantly accompanied her for counseling because, as he said, "she threatened to leave me if I did not."

The history that unfolded was that of a man emotionally unresponsive to his partner's feelings, while Anne had experienced years of frustration trying to draw out some passion from Stephen. The expression of feelings was foreign to him. When asked the question: "How does that make you feel?" Stephen would exhibit a mild, quizzical look, and respond, "I really don't know." At first I thought he did not want to reveal his emotions. However, after some further probing, I realized he was really trying to express himself on a feeling level but could not. It was a skill he did not have. Stephen could talk about what he was thinking, yet he was at a loss for words when asked to describe his own emotional inner world. He really tried.

Fortunately, Stephen kept trying. Anne learned that he was not purposely withholding his feelings from her, but had learned from an early age to repress them. Over time he learned to become more aware of his inner feelings. He also gained the confidence to share some of his fears and desires with Anne. Granted, today I would not describe Stephen as an emotionally expressive person; however, just a little means a lot to Anne. They have discovered a degree of safety and security that comes from an emotional connection, a connection that was missing from their relationship. Their future looks brighter.

Our Changing Roles

For some time now, women have taken on what used to be considered a "man's world." Some of these women, after much hard work and struggle, are reaching the top levels of the corporate ladder. Many are becoming business owners and are changing the traditional model of a businessperson. Most are retaining their personal emotional lives, and that is good news. Unfortunately, some are not.

I have worked with female clients who exhibited a lack of skill in expressing their emotions. Take the case of Janet. It seems as if, in her eagerness to make it in the corporate world, Janet had adopted the

traditional "unemotional" male role. She also claimed to have been taught since childhood not to show emotions, in a similar way to many males. Janet had few female friends, and even fewer with whom she shared an emotional connection. At first she had been pleased with her ability to stand her ground with "the boys." However, she had become aware that there was something missing in her life. She had been in an intimate relationship for three years with a man, named Brent, whom she portrayed as being very caring and kind. "Most of the time he's more emotional than I am." The problem, as she described it, was that Brent wanted her to express her feelings more openly.

This case was in many ways similar to the case of "the emotionless man," only in this instance it was a woman. Today we can no longer write about relationships between men and women in the traditional way, even though my experience has shown that there are significantly more unemotional men than women. The good news is that the number of men who are open to their emotions, especially among the younger generation, is increasing. You might say these men are discovering their nurturing side. This is especially true with those men who stay home to take care of the children.

When our first granddaughter, Sarah, was born, Dean was the one who took maternity leave, while June returned to her work of teaching nursing. This experience was a very rewarding one for both Sarah and Dean. The special bond that developed between the two of them was wonderful to watch. Twenty months later, when Emily and Mackenzie were born, and June opted to stay home, a beautiful balance existed in the family. Both partners shared equally in the physical and emotional lives of their children.

Today those men who share the responsibility of raising the children equally with their partner are showing a positive trend to being more open with their feelings, a trend that is being applauded by many women. This positive trend will hopefully continue, for men and women alike, now that it is becoming more fashionable in the workplace to be in touch with our emotions.

A healthy relationship is one where both partners are "emotionally intelligent."

It's All About Love

Just how much an emotional connection matters for a healthy relationship, really became clear to me on November 4, 1996. That was the day I was participating in another five-day intensive training program for counseling couples. It was also the day I met Susan M. Johnson. Dr. Johnson, as one of the leaders of this program, influenced the way I have worked with couples ever since. Her presentation on Emotionally Focused Therapy (EFT) for couples gave me a big piece of the puzzle, and convinced me of its effectiveness as a couple's counseling approach. I came away with a counseling tool that provided a realistic and powerful lens to view how couples bond.

Continued training in this area has given me a better understanding of how we make intimate commitments on an emotional level. We make these commitments because we love and need each other. As Dr. Johnson states in her book *Creating Connection:* "Seeking and maintaining contact with others is a primary motivating principle in human beings." Secure attachment is healthy and provides a safe environment for us to develop as individuals. Adult love is seen as a bond or an emotional tie with an intimate partner, and wanting a source of comfort, care and protection is healthy and desirable. The ideal relationship is one that provides a secure base from which to confront the world.

EFT is still a fairly new approach for helping distressed couples; yet, it is considered by many experts to be the best current theoretical model for understanding adult relationships. For those of you who are wondering how successful it is, let me just say that it has been proven as one of the few clinically effective couple therapies. I am finding it extremely helpful with different couples, including those in which individual partners suffer from significant problems.

Building a secure attachment has become my primary focus in couple's counseling. My focus is on helping to create the kind of connection that brings health and happiness for couples, that will withstand any challenge to the partnership, and will lead to greater intimacy and joy.

Turmoil ensues when our relationship is threatened. When our source of comfort and protection is in danger, we can start to panic. We want to do whatever it takes to protect it. Unfortunately, we often do the kinds of things that have the opposite effect on our relationship. Instead of creating a stronger connection, we can start to detach and distance ourselves from our partner. The fear of losing our connection can cause us to stop looking for, and giving support to, our partner.

To protect ourselves we may incorrectly begin to distrust, and withdraw from, the security we so desperately need.

Fear of Detachment

Separation anxiety may be the primary fear of childhood; however, this fear still exists in us as adults. It might not be as life-threatening, but the intensity of this fear can still overwhelm us. When the security of our intimate relationship is in danger, the fear we experience can stir up desperate behaviors.

This fear is sometimes used to motivate a partner to change their behavior. I can attest to the fact that the threat of detachment is often used by one partner to convince his or her mate to come in for counseling. Threats like, "If you're not willing to work on this problem I'm leaving you," can be a strong motivator. It is unfortunate that many couples wait until their problems have reached a critical stage before they seek out help. What they don't realize is that sometimes it is the fear of detachment that is actually holding their partner back from going for counseling. The unwilling partner is often afraid that their problems are insurmountable, and that the only possible result of

going to counseling will be separation. Some of these reluctant individuals even incorrectly assume that their partner will be advised to leave them. When asked about this assumption, the response I have received is, "You see it all the time on those talk shows. People are being told to stop putting up with any crap and just leave."

I am not suggesting here that a person who is being abused should stay. In fact, I encourage any person who is experiencing any form of abuse to seek professional help. I will also direct an abusive partner to get help for their problem, and to realize that their abusive behavior is going to result in them losing the very person they need.

What I am suggesting is that we need to be aware of how our attachment concerns cause our sometimes bizarre and desperate behaviors. The fear and hurt we experience can trigger responses such as angry outbursts, feelings of despair, clinging behavior, avoidance and isolation. The goal of couple's counseling is to help loving partners to recognize these reactions and to understand their need for safety, security and respect, to deal with the fear of detachment, and to promote the creation of a secure and loving bond.

I firmly believe that there is too much "leaving" going on, and not enough "staying to work it out." Too many people are suffering from loneliness and depression, and have become dependent on antidepressants and other mood-altering drugs. The answer lies in the creation of more secure and healthy relationships.

The healing power of a loving relationship can never be overstated.

The Green-eyed Monster

When was the last time you experienced a queasy, sick-to-your-stomach feeling? I'm not asking about flu symptoms here, but that painful reaction you feel when you become afraid of losing your

partner to another person. It's called jealousy. It can feel worse than the flu. The experience of it can cause you to become anxious and defensive, and in some cases to lose control. Real or imagined, justified or not, there are few feelings that can be as painful as the ones caused by jealousy. Many people describe feeling physically sick—not being able to eat—and walking around feeling miserable.

There are many types of jealousy. Jealousy means different things to different people, and people's reactions to it can be just as varied. Each type of jealousy involves the fear of losing something precious. You might be jealous about your partner's work because it takes time away from the moments you might have spent together. Jealousy of sports, hobbies, outside interests, or anything that takes away the attention you want from your loved one, can wake up the old "monster." However, the one that is the hardest to bear is *sexual jealousy*. Sexual jealousy is perhaps the most painful emotion we know, because it threatens our self-worth as well as the strength of our most personal and private connection.

Think back to the last time you were at a party. Did you experience any threat to your relationship when you saw your partner chatting with an attractive guest? If so, you probably felt more than simple displeasure. You might have experienced a flash of hate towards the guest, your partner and even yourself. Let's face it, moments like that can overwhelm you. Fear of losing your partner, and all their love and affection, can be a terrifying feeling. There's no doubt about it—jealousy hurts.

Jealousy *Can* Bring You Closer

Many people believe that jealousy is unhealthy and destructive, or that it is a sign of a bad relationship. The truth is that jealousy is a signal of a potential problem. When handled properly, it can actually serve to bring us closer to our partner.

The interesting thing I have discovered about jealousy is that there is a real division among the experts as to whether jealousy is normal or abnormal. They are also split in their opinion about jealousy being instinctive or learned. There is agreement, however, that jealousy is universal and that it is meant to be a warning. Most agree that as a basic emotion, it acts as a signal to warn us that we could lose something we value.

Regardless of whether jealousy is instinctive or learned, normal or abnormal, most of us have experienced it. What I believe is important, is how we respond when we think our relationship is threatened. Reacting with verbal cruelty, physical attacks, running away or long periods of paranoia and suspicion, is destructive to us and to the relationship. On the other hand, not reacting in any way and claiming that you never get jealous also may be an indication of something wrong. Hiding your feelings of jealousy can breed resentment and suspicion, and be destructive and harmful to your relationship.

Jealousy can also provide a clue as to how you feel about yourself and your partner. If you depend solely on your partner for most of your emotional needs, and you have feelings of low self-worth, you can be extremely susceptible to jealousy. The more you value yourself, the less likely it is that you will feel jealous.

I believe that jealousy is not necessarily a sign of unhealthy possessiveness or a serious character flaw. Providing you handle it appropriately, jealousy can create personal growth and revitalize your relationship. Sharing your jealous feelings can be constructive, and can help to heal unresolved feelings and bring you and your partner closer together.

For Colleen, the green-eyed monster had been causing her to feel unhappy for many years. It had also created some painful moments for Kevin, her partner for the past six years. The problem had actually begun during the first years of their relationship. Colleen explained that they met each other at a party and were immediately attracted to each other. Kevin described how, during their first year together, they grew closer and closer, and began exploring the possibility of moving in together. And then it happened. Colleen recalled the painful moment when she found out that "Kevin slept with another woman. Just a month before we were going to move in together he ends up having sex with someone else."

Kevin explained: "I felt so guilty about what I had done that I just had to tell Colleen. I wanted her to understand that it was just sex. It meant nothing. I guess I just wanted to experience it with another person before we committed ourselves to each other."

"I was so hurt by what he did," said Colleen. "Eventually I was able to forgive him, and four months later we moved in together."

The problem was that this painful experience remained as unfinished business. Anytime Colleen saw Kevin even look sideways at another woman, she would react with anger. And even though, as Kevin explained it, "I've never been unfaithful to her since that day, she still gets upset, even if it's just a business lunch with a client."

The problem was that Colleen had not healed the wounds of that painful moment. The experience was still creating fear and causing hurt. What was necessary was for both of them to express their complete range of feelings and to truly understand what that meant for them.

The healing began when Kevin was able to empathize with Colleen and understand the pain his infidelity had caused. His taking responsibility for his act of betrayal also helped Colleen to understand his commitment to their relationship, and that he truly cared for her. They came to understand that they were still very much attached, and that the fear of detachment was causing these strong and sometimes painful reactions. Their ability to empathize with each other allowed them to connect and establish a greater sense of security. Being honest with each other and sharing their innermost feelings led to a sense of trust that reignited their love for each other.

When you are emotionally connected and you feel secure in your relationship, you will be less afraid of the old "green-eyed monster."

Reflect

Reflect on the emotional intimacy and the closeness that exists in your loving relationship. Do you experience a sense of connection and security, and a deep emotional bond? Are you authentic and open with your partner? Think about your relationship and how it is affected by your ability to share your innermost feelings.

What do you need to do to increase the emotional intimacy and the feeling of closeness? Are you taking responsibility for the level of security and emotional connection in your relationship? Jot down a few notes about what you can do, and what you want to accomplish.

Me

____

____

____

____

____

____

____

____

My Partner

____

____

____

____

____

____

____

____

A Beautiful Balance

A beautiful balance exists in your life when you and your loving partner are able to experience a sense of emotional and physical connection. Connection is really the "core" of the seven "C"s. It is the heart of the relationship. Your ability to care, change, communicate, deal with conflict, be creative and make a commitment, will determine the amount of comfort, closeness and protection. It is a loving relationship when two people experience a feeling of closeness, security and a deep emotional bond.

Make a commitment to continue and improve the level of security and connection in your relationship. List what you will do in the space below. Work together as loving partners to develop your list. Choose what you consider to be the most important behavior you need to strengthen, to create a secure and healthy relationship. Transfer this choice to your self-contract at the end of this book.

Me

____

____

____

____

____

____

My Partner

____

____

____

____

____

____

Conflict

Conflict can help to resolve the hurts and differences between loving partners.

The Threat

"I get so mad sometimes that I feel like walking out and never coming back."

Couples have often come to see me because they are so mad at each other they can't seem to get past the anger.

When I ask them my usual opening question, "How can I help?" the usual response I get is: "We want you to help us to stop fighting." My next statement is then often met with surprise: "If I did that, I would not be helping you. Conflict is a normal part of an intimate relationship. It can rarely be avoided, and in fact, it should not be avoided."

When it comes to conflict between loving partners, it is not about stopping the fights; instead, it is about learning to "fight fair." Before I discuss how to fight fair, let me dispel three common myths about conflict.

Myth #1: We should suppress our bad feelings and avoid expressing our anger.

Myth #2: Loving partners don't fight.

Myth #3: When an intimate couple fight a lot, it means that their relationship will not last.

Let me start by dispelling the first myth, about suppressing our feelings of anger, with this basic truth: Keeping your mouth shut and not expressing your anger will only lead to more problems. A tremendous amount of psychological research, as well as our own common sense, tells us that avoiding problems is not the answer. In his book *After the Fight: Using Your Disagreements to Build a Stronger Relationship,* Daniel Wile states, "We can keep our mouths shut, but that just leads to a loss of feeling for our partners, and often to bad feelings and fights anyway when what we have suppressed eventually pops out." Dr. Wile, who is one of the most respected psychologists in the field of dealing with couples in conflict, points out that problems arise "from our unavoidable failures to get across what we feel."

Unfortunately, many of us have been taught that the expression of anger is wrong. As children, we were told to "calm down," or cautioned, "Don't you ever act that way again." We were given a very strong message that we were wrong for letting this bad feeling out. Few of us were told that anger can be a constructive emotion. In fact, anger can help to resolve the hurts and differences between loving partners. It can make our relationship stronger. The key is learning how to fight fair and expressing your anger in an appropriate way. Perhaps Aristotle, in *The Nicomachean Ethics,* said it best: "Anyone can become angry—that is easy. But to be angry with the right person, to the right degree, at the right time, for the right purpose, and in the right way—that is not easy."

Dealing with conflict and anger isn't easy because few of us have

ever received any training on how to do it effectively. Isn't it interesting that when it comes to two of the major problems we experience in our intimate relationships, active listening and conflict resolution, we have never received any formal training?

The second myth that "loving partners don't fight" is another one that I suggest you stop believing. As James L. Creighton says about this myth, in his excellent book *How Loving Couples Fight,* "A part of nearly everyone, even those of us with professional training, stubbornly clings to this falsehood." Dr. Creighton also points out the years of research that have revealed that, "In the most successful relationships, the partners neither avoid conflict nor look upon it as particularly threatening. On the contrary, they accept it as normal and healthy."

These successful couples have realized that a healthy relationship means that at times you can and you do disagree, and sometimes you struggle and hurt. They do not delude themselves into believing that the best relationship is one that is stress-free and full of peace and tranquility. They realize that to believe in that type of relationship is to believe in fairy tales. It's ironic that lately we have seen a number of biographies about actors who have portrayed ideal relationships and families on screen, while in reality their lives were far from what they projected. Sadly, many of us still continue to believe in these fictional portrayals. We feel disappointed and wish that we could have such an idyllic relationship, not realizing it's a hoax.

The third myth, that when an intimate couple fight a lot it means that their relationship will not last, is another one that needs to be challenged. In reality, the quantity and level of your disagreements is no predictor of the length of your relationship. I have known and worked with couples that had disagreements on a regular basis. I have even had some couples express pride in the fact that they had regular fights. They considered their relationship to be a good one and claimed they had grown closer and more secure over the years. These couples often were quick to add that, regardless of the quantity of their disagreements, they loved each other. The main difference I see between these couples and the ones that do break up, is that they truly care for each other. The couples that are on the verge of ending their relationship usually display a lack of caring. They often show disrespect and even contempt for their partner, and this is, I believe, the difference between a secure relationship and one that is on shaky ground.

A secure relationship has nothing to do with the amount of conflict, but everything to do with how the individuals in the relationship fight and the kind of respect they show for each other. These individuals also have a healthy respect for themselves. In other words, they feel good about themselves and have a high degree of self-worth. What is also common to all of these loving and secure couples is that they consider their relationship to be important enough to work on improving it.

We all have our own ideas about what makes a great relationship. And when we begin to experience more conflict than we are comfortable with, which for many people means the least amount possible, we begin to fear that our relationship is in trouble. I recall reading some years ago about the work being done by Dr. George R. Bach. Dr. Bach, together with Peter Wyden, wrote a book called *The Intimate Enemy: How to Fight Fair in Love and Marriage.* In this book the authors revealed "the art of fighting right," and suggested that it is most often the tendency of couples to try and avoid a fight that leads to more trouble. Demands like, "Don't get angry with me!" or "Don't raise your voice—or else!" can, in fact, cause escalation of the conflict. Their results demonstrate that couples tended "to feel closest after a properly fought fight." The key word here is "properly."

It is very important to point out that any form of abuse, either verbal or physical, is never acceptable. Emotional abuse can be as destructive and painful as physical abuse. You can learn to fight fair, without using mean or hurtful words or hitting someone. Being abusive to your partner should never be justified or seen as fair.

So there you have it. Conflict is normal and unavoidable in an intimate partnership. You can have a healthy relationship and still have conflict. Fighting fair can even make your relationship stronger. The answer lies in developing ways to express and resolve your differences, while still respecting yourself and your partner. Once you have the skills to fight fairly, you will no longer avoid conflict. Learning how to deal with your conflicts means that you will no longer feel threatened by them. This can be empowering.

Conflict can help to resolve the hurts and differences between loving partners.

It's OK to Go to Bed Angry

You're probably wondering if this heading is a misprint. So many times you have heard the statement, "Don't go to bed angry." Well, I agree with this rule for some people, but not for others. Some people just are not able to get rid of their angry feelings as quickly as others. They need time to think it through, and resolve some issues on their own and on their own time. Others seem to operate in a different time zone and are more comfortable discussing difficult issues at certain times that are not acceptable to others. I'll admit that, initially, I believed this rule of not going to bed angry. I think a lot had to do with the fact that I consider myself a night person. I would be willing to discuss and resolve an issue at three in the morning. Susan on the other hand would like nothing better than to sleep at that time and resolve the issue the next day.

There is another factor that this rule does not take into account. Some people are what you might call "slow burners." They do get angry, but not so quickly. They also take longer to process and resolve their anger. Some others are fast processors or "hot burners." What that means is that one person can get angry in a flash, and get

over it just as quickly, while another will be slower to react and needs time to work it through in his or her own mind.

Being a fast processor, or hot burner, is not necessarily a good thing. Don't compare this to a computer where we want the fastest processor available. The fast processors may get over their anger quickly but they are often the first to *get* angry. So they may trigger a fight and then leave the slow burners wondering what happened. I think the "not going to bed angry" rule must have been written by a fast processor.

Researchers suggest that there is a genetic inclination for how quickly we become angry and then get over our anger. However, genetic inclination or not, you can still adjust your fighting style. If you find that the way you fight is causing more problems than it is solving, you can explore and develop a style that works better for you and your relationship. The key is to work at it before you experience a major fight. Practice your new approach during the lesser conflicts, and get comfortable with your new behavior. That way, when it really counts, you will feel in control, without being controlling. You'll be able to deal with conflict in a more productive way.

Loving partners who respect each other are able to turn away from each other and agree on a place and time to deal with the conflict the next day. They know from experience that having a fight and disagreeing is not a threat to the health of their relationship.

Loving partners also know that sometimes it is best to think it through and come back to resolve the conflict when your mind is clear and you are well rested.

The Case of the Screamer

Dr. John Gottman is another researcher who has done extensive work in the area of conflict and the factors that make a relationship succeed

or fail. In his book *The Seven Principles for Making Marriage Work*, co-written with Nan Silver, he states, "Even happily married couples can have screaming matches—loud arguments don't necessarily harm a marriage." I am not suggesting, however, that this research means it is OK to yell and scream at your partner, especially if your partner has real difficulty handling the intensity of your outburst.

Take the case of David and Lori. They had been experiencing many fights during their five-year marriage, and both felt frustrated with the fact that many of their recent fights had gone unresolved. Lori expressed her concern that some of these fights actually frightened her. When I questioned Lori about the fear, she responded that, "It reminds me of the vicious fights between my parents. Especially when dad would come home drunk." The problem was that when David started to scream, it triggered Lori's fear that the fight might lead to abuse. She revealed, "Whenever I think the fighting is getting too intense, I get scared and try to stop it before it escalates."

David described a family where, as the youngest of six children, yelling was the only way he could ensure he'd be heard. For him it was a normal way to argue. However, he did admit that the degree and level of his yelling had turned into screaming. "Lately I've noticed that my throat hurts after one of these fights." He expressed his frustration about being told not to yell before the fight even started, and revealed that when he believed Lori would not listen to his concerns, he would react in his old, childhood way. David confessed that he would "yell even louder when Lori tells me to stop screaming," because he thought she was just trying to cut him off. He agreed to tone it down.

Eventually the fights became less fearful for Lori, as David became more aware of, and was able to lower, his level of "screaming" behavior. Lori, for her part, was more willing to remain and "discuss the issues." The less frequently she ran away, the less often he yelled. The less frequently he yelled, the less often she ran away.

Here again we see the power of taking responsibility for our own behavior. The first step is being aware of what we are doing and the effect it is having on our relationship. However, just as we explored in Chapter 2: Change, it is up to you to take responsibility for changing yourself without trying to change your partner. I recognize that when it comes to fighting it is often both partners who contribute to the escalation. And even though one person may be more responsible than the other, it is helpful for at least one of you to adjust your behavior.

In David and Lori's case, they each took some responsibility, and they each cared for and respected the other, which resulted in quicker de-escalation in their fighting behavior. I want to point out that even if only David had adjusted his behavior, it would have caused de-escalation as well. This change in his behavior would cause Lori to be less fearful of a potential fight. She would then be more willing to deal with the problem, resulting in David becoming less fearful that he was going to be ignored.

Certainly David and Lori are likely to have some screaming matches. They are human after all. However, as all the research suggests, **loving couples who have a strong and healthy relationship can have an occasional fight where they ignore all the rules and still survive.**

Who's Really Responsible?

Most often when we are upset at our partner we insist that "they are responsible" for our anger. Statements like, "He makes me so mad!" or, "She really gets me upset whenever she talks to me in *that tone*," are very common. If you can relate to these statements, and you often hear yourself saying them, then you need to understand a basic concept that will help you deal with your anger and reduce the number of times you get yourself upset. You need to understand and accept that there is no way another person can make you mad or upset. In fact, no person, no thing, no event, no external situation, not even your partner, can get you angry or upset or distressed. *You*

upset yourself. Now I realize that's a pretty strong statement. Clients have been known to get mad at me for saying this. Even so, I believe it, and I've been saying it for over 20 years. Before that, I would have also blamed somebody else when I got upset.

Now, if you're asking, "How do I get *myself* so upset?" the answer I always give is, "Through your own *thinking*, your belief system, your own point of view." It is our *thinking* that determines our *feelings* and *actions*. I first began to truly understand this concept when I read a little booklet entitled *A Rational Counseling Primer,* written by Howard Young. In it, Howard made the statement that, "People…are not disturbed by things, but by views which they take of things." This idea, I discovered later on, was not new. In the 1st century A.D., Greek philosopher Epictetus stated: "Men are disturbed not by things, but by the views which they take of them." Some centuries later, Shakespeare wrote in *Hamlet*: "There is nothing either good or bad, but thinking makes it so." So you see, the idea that we upset ourselves is not new. We've known about it for centuries, you might even say for millennia. Even though we have known about this, we like to ignore the facts. It is so much easier to blame somebody else and make them responsible for our anger.

But just because something is easier doesn't mean it's right. The truth is that our beliefs create our reality. What you believe about an event will determine how you respond to it. It all comes down to the fact that human beings have the unique capacity and ability to think and reason. According to several experts (Albert Ellis, Aaron Beck and Donald Meichenbaum, among others), self-talk plays an important role in people's coping skills, how we get angry and how we fight. Unfortunately, we also have a tendency to use negative self-talk, which can become automatic over time. It is as if we have a program in our brain that starts to run when a particular button is pushed. Since the things we say to ourselves about a situation will have a direct result on how we feel and then behave, it is tremendously important that we become aware of our own belief systems, our own programming.

Let me present a brief illustration by using a simple A.B.C. method developed by Albert Ellis. For a detailed description of this method, I recommend you read Dr. Ellis's excellent book, *A New Guide to Rational Living.* This simple system is based on the premise that when **something happens,** such as your partner criticizes you, that triggers your **attitude** or **belief** about the criticism, which in turn creates your **reaction as a result of your belief**.

A. **Activating Event:** Your partner says, "I hate to remind you again, but would you please turn that off?"
B. **Beliefs or Thoughts:** Your program is activated. "There's that nagging again. It's just too much. I can't stand it."
C. **Consequence or Emotional Reaction:** You feel angry, or depressed or even hostile.

It is not the event, but rather it is your interpretation of it, that causes your emotional reaction and consequent behavior.

The more extreme our point of view about what our partner does or says, the more intensely we will feel about it. Let me give an example: If I were to tell Susan, "You know, you're just like your mother," well, some of you might be thinking, "Boy, is he in for it." And I suppose for some of you that might be just what would happen. If your partner interprets your comment as a criticism, you might find yourself in a fight. However, in my case, I happen to really like and respect my mother-in-law. She is a very kind and generous person, whom I admire greatly. Susan knows I feel this way about her, and would therefore take my comment as a compliment rather than a criticism.

The problems that surface in relationships, however, often occur when we know each other's "hot buttons" and we push them anyway. Let's assume a similar scenario, as above, but in this case you know that your partner has some strong negative feelings about her mother. In a moment of weakness you make the accusation, "You're

just like your mother!" And of course, you get back what you expected. Your partner feels anger as a result of your criticism. Now, based on what I have said about how our own thinking is responsible for our feelings, you might say, "I'm not responsible. It is my partner's programming, or belief system, that caused this negative reaction." Well, in this case, I would suggest you could take responsibility for the outcome. As intimate partners, we get to know each other's hot buttons, and just like a computer, whenever we push these buttons, we get a predictable response.

The ideal is that we each become aware of our belief systems and our own "hot buttons" and learn to reprogram them. So the next time our partner pushes that button, we might surprise them by responding with, "Thank you. That's very nice of you to say that." Before you start thinking that the suggestion here is to suppress our emotions, let's be clear. This is not about becoming a computer and not expressing our feelings. It is about becoming aware of our emotions, understanding them and learning to deal with them appropriately.

We need to understand that anger is not something that happens *to* us. It is our own thinking and our own interpretation that creates our reaction. So the next time you get yourself upset by making a negative interpretation, see if you can identify your negative self-talk. Determine how your thoughts are responsible for your emotional upset. Take responsibility and go to the next step, which is to **dispute** and **question** your negative self-talk. Whenever you can change your thinking, you will always create a **new effect** and **emotion**. Expanding on the A.B.C. example, you could do the following:

D. **Disputing negative self-talk:** You could say to yourself, "Maybe turning it off is a good idea. I have been ignoring my partner and I can see how frustrating that is. Perhaps it isn't nagging, but a plea for some closeness or attention."

E. **New effect or emotion:** Accepting that your partner has a legitimate concern. Knowing that the more you resist, the worse it gets, will help you to change your thinking, which in turn will change your reaction.

A change in mind will result in a change in feelings—even knowing that, as discussed in Chapter 4: Connection, the more we are attached to our partner the more intense our reactions will be. There is some truth in the words of that old song, "You always hurt the one you love." We know that the more deeply we feel for each other, the greater the chance for hurt and conflict.

We also know that the more we care for each other, the greater the chance for healing and joy.

The Self-fulfilling Prophecy

Understanding the power of your own thinking, and knowing how it can affect your behavior, is an important step in dealing with conflict. It is also important to understand how your self-concept, how you see yourself and your expectations, can affect when and how you fight.

Through our own thinking, and what we expect will happen, we can actually affect the outcome of a situation. It is called a self-fulfilling prophecy. We do it all the time, especially when it comes to how we fight. For example:

- You anticipate that bringing up a difficult issue will result in a fight and your expectation comes true.
- You expect to get angry if your partner reminds you about something you forgot, and you do.
- You say you are not going to like a certain discussion and, sure enough, you don't.

Whenever you believe and predict that something is going to turn

out badly, there is a good chance that you make it turn out that way. You help make it happen. Think about a time you had to make a presentation and you said to yourself, "I'm sure I'm going to blow this." How did you feel? Did it give you confidence, or did you end up forgetting things? Most likely it was the latter. Your prediction comes true because your self-concept influences your behavior, and you start doing those old familiar things that lead to the same old familiar outcomes. As Henry Ford once said, "If you think you can or can't, you are right."

I'm sure you've had the experience of seeing a certain look on your partner's face and thinking, "This is going to be a bad fight." Once you have decided on the outcome, you start acting in a way that makes it come true.

Accordingly, use the power of your predictions and turn them into positive expectations. And by that I don't mean saying, "I'm positive we're going to have a bad fight." I mean turning around your negative expectations and self-concept. You may be pleasantly surprised at the results once you start believing that you will have a good outcome from your disagreements. If you want to break a negative cycle, believing that you can do it is the most important thing. I cannot overemphasize the importance of maintaining a positive outlook.

The next time you find yourself getting depressed or unmotivated after a particularly frustrating argument, remember that **there is ample evidence that your own thinking and expectation affected the result.**

Resistance Is Futile!

If you are familiar with the above statement, you know it comes from the "Star Trek" series. It is made by the "Borg" whenever they sense resistance from a species they are attempting to assimilate. They simply inform them that there is no point in struggling because

it won't make any difference. There is a lesson in that statement. How often do we find ourselves struggling with and resisting something that we simply cannot change? How often have you found yourself in a conflict with your partner, and the harder you tried to resolve it the more intense it got? Unfortunately many of us will answer "too often." Our usual response is to rely on our old coping skills and just try a little harder. Now be truthful, has that worked for you? "Well obviously not," you might say, "or I wouldn't be experiencing the escalation of the conflict." It's just like famous coach Vince Lombardi once said, "Just because you're doing something wrong, doing it more intensely isn't going to help."

Beating your head against a brick wall is not going to hurt the wall, but it will surely cause you pain. Sometimes the only answer is to find your inner peace and not try to control something over which you have no control. It always helps to remember that the only thing you have control over is yourself and your own thinking. You cannot control your partner. Unfortunately, many of us try to do exactly that. As in the A.B.C. method previously illustrated, how often can you change or control *the activating event*? The answer is, not very often, if ever. Yet, here we are constantly trying to change A when we would be so much better off if we focused on B, beliefs or thoughts. Perhaps it will be helpful to remind ourselves about the well-known serenity prayer, "God grant me the *serenity* to accept the things I cannot change, the *courage* to change the things I can, and the *wisdom* to know the difference."

At times, the best, if not the only, way to handle a situation is to stop struggling. You have heard the saying, "Go with the flow." The saying I like best is actually the title of a book by Barry Stevens: *Don't Push the River*. As the title suggests, you may be a rock or a dam, but it doesn't matter because no matter how hard you try to stop it, the river will find a way around you. Continuing with this metaphoric approach, think about swimming together with your partner. If something should happen and you start to drown, it is always best that you relax

and stop struggling. The more you panic and struggle, the worse the situation gets, and you and your partner could both go down.

All this is not to suggest that you simply give in or give up communicating. It is to remind us that we can become obsessive about something and forget that, at times, the only answer is to let go, take a deep breath and find some inner peace. A good example of this is the increasing occurrence of "road rage" on our highways. Too often we make the dangerous assumption that the person who cut us off is responsible for our anger. We can then escalate our stupidity by chasing after the supposed offender. And we often justify our actions by thinking, "It's not my fault. It's that stupid idiot who didn't even look in the mirror and almost caused a major accident. I should teach him a lesson!" Next thing you know you're barreling down the road, endangering yourself and everyone else who has the misfortune to be in your path. In this type of situation, we may not even realize that we are not really teaching anyone a lesson; we are just trying to get even. The best lesson would be to show others that we can remain calm even when we are frightened or frustrated.

Imagine if you found yourself in a similar incident and after being cut off, you could change your self-talk to something like, "Boy that was close. I'm glad I was able to react quickly and not cause a collision. I may have been in that driver's blind spot. No harm, no foul." Believe me, it is so much better for everyone involved. I should know. I have been the chaser and the chased.

Stopping ourselves from behaving in self-defeating yet familiar ways is not always easy. However, you learned that behavior in the first place, so you can also unlearn it. It takes a conscious effort, hard work and practice. Understanding the theory is not enough. You will need to repeatedly challenge and discover your self-defeating thinking and replace it with constructive and positive ideas. Eventually it becomes habit-forming, just like your old familiar ways. So the next time you find yourself in your partner's "blind spot," meaning they are not intending to get you upset or cause you harm, a good response might be to take a deep breath, be aware of your self-talk, and try not to escalate the conflict. Instead, resolve it.

I will confess that I love driving cars. Now before you say that's a guy thing, let me just say I have met many women who feel the same way. In my case, I used to race formula cars, and for a while was quite good at it. Back in 1971, I won the Canadian National Championship. By 1974 I had won four more regional championships, as well as the prestigious "Driver to Europe" award. Unfortunately, or as Susan says now "fortunately," Canadians were not well known as race-car drivers back then. We were known for our hockey, but the rest of the world was not familiar with our active and very competitive racing program. Without an agent and sufficient sponsorship money, I decided to retire and returned to Canada, never to race again.

A year later I met Susan. After dating for a few weeks, I decided to impress this lady (now, *that* could be a guy thing), so I invited her to go with me to watch a race at Mosport. I figured that I'd show her around and explain the finer details of "clipping the apex," "under steering" and "drifting" through the turns. Things seemed to be going quite well as I introduced her to some of the officials who informed her of my past accomplishments. Too soon, it was time to drive home. And then it hit me. I could really impress this lady by actually showing her my driving skills. I should mention that by this time I had returned to school and was a poor student who did not own a car. However, my former sponsor had kindly supplied me with a loaner. The loaner was an Audi. Susan had taken one look at this car and said, "That's just like the car my dad used to have. It's a Rambler, isn't it?" Well, that should have been my first clue that Susan didn't know too much about cars, but I motored on, as they say.

Now imagine, here I am in my glory, a well-engineered and beautifully performing automotive creation in my hands, and a perfect location to show off my skills. Life couldn't be better. I'm pushing

the pedal to the floor, drifting through the corners, with the steering wheel playing beneath my hands. I'm thinking, "If this doesn't impress her, I don't know what will." I look over, with pride in my eyes and see...horror in Susan's. Not only is Susan not impressed, she's petrified. Her fear turns to anger, and before I know it we're having our first major fight. Talk about different perceptions! I was seeing myself as the skilled driver, showing off my prowess; she was seeing me as an idiot, endangering her life.

How many of you reading this scenario have had fights about your partner's driving? I'm sure quite a few. I share this example with you because driving has been a source of conflict with a number of my clients. During the earlier years of our relationship, it had also been an issue between Susan and myself. I have always considered myself a safe and defensive driver. I have never had, nor to my knowledge caused, an accident. However, I will admit that I sometimes drive over the speed limit and that it took a while to adjust my driving to Susan's comfort level.

The answer to our problem wasn't so much compromise as it was achieving a win-win solution. With compromise, one or sometimes both partners give up something. And this giving up can sometimes leave one or both partners disappointed. If you look up the meaning of compromise in *Webster's Dictionary*, you will read, "To settle by making mutual concessions." After trying different forms of compromise, Susan and I still felt dissatisfied. I even suggested Susan drive, and for a while she had her own car. We soon discovered this was a lose-lose situation, resulting in both of us not enjoying the experience. She doesn't like driving, and I am more comfortable when I'm behind the wheel. Of course I could have suggested that Susan get over her fear by accepting that I was a safe driver with no accidents to my record. That solution, however, would have been a win-lose. And that means one of us, in this case Susan, would have come up short.

Eventually we were able to sort out our problem. Whenever Susan experiences any discomfort as a passenger, she will express her con-

cern *without being critical of my driving*. I am also willing to make the driving experience pleasant for both of us. I will drive at a safe and comfortable speed that does not exceed her comfort level. Since I do most of the driving, and Susan is not really into cars, I get to choose the type and model of car we own. The last time we bought a car I almost thought I would be making a major concession. I have always enjoyed a car with manual transmission, while Susan prefers an automatic. We had agreed that she would be driving the car more often, especially on long trips, so the automatic was the preferred choice. To my pleasant surprise, these new computer-controlled transmissions are really neat. I actually enjoy them even more than a manual transmission. We both experienced a win-win.

The issue of who drives, and how they drive, has long been a source of conflict for many couples. I have seen couples who were on the brink of breaking up because of their "driving fights." The driving itself wasn't really the source of their potential breakup. The problem was their inability to reach a win-win solution. A win-win is only achieved when both partners' needs and interests are satisfied. It does not involve one person using power to win over the other, and win at the other's expense. Nor does it involve compromise where both partners may feel they are losing. Win-win involves negotiations based on trust, with open disclosure. Winning partners also genuinely care for themselves and their partner.

Resolving conflicts between loving partners is not a competitive sport.

What About Money?

Money is another major issue for many couples. The same principles that apply to resolving other conflicts can be applied here as well. In other words, make it a win-win situation.

If you find yourselves frequently fighting over the budget, or the lack of one, you will need to discuss what each of you want and need. The next step is to think about and "brainstorm" as many solutions as you can to satisfy your individual needs. Once you have chosen the best solutions that satisfy you both, make it happen.

Agreeing on a budget, and where the money will be spent, is one solution. Each of you having some money of your own to do with as you wish, could be another solution. Even deciding who will be responsible for keeping and monitoring the budget could be an important issue. It may not be easy, and it takes some time, but it is well worth the effort if you both feel satisfied.

Sometimes it takes a disagreement to bring the real issues to the surface. For example, the conflict may not be about money, instead it may really be about control. After all, money is a symbol of control in our culture. Take the time to discover and share what is really concerning you. Perhaps it was best said by Hugh Prather in his lovely book *Notes to Myself:* "Our marriage used to suffer from arguments that were too short. Now we argue long enough to find out what the argument is about."

Those Little Irritants

Have you ever wondered why a simple little irritant can cause a major blow-up? Or something you used to think was cute is now making you cringe? Well, it could be because you are letting little events pile up and accumulate until they have become a major problem. You may be collecting these minor irritants and bottling them up until the pressure gets too much, and you explode.

You are not alone. Many partners store these incidents away, and save them for something really big. Unfortunately, it can take just one too many of these little irritants to lead to a blow-up. This concept was wonderfully illustrated in a book written in the 1970s by

Richard Lessor entitled *Love & Marriage and Trading Stamps.* Back then, it was very popular for people to cash in their books of trading stamps, collected from purchases, in exchange for prizes like goods or services. Today we collect stamps from certain fast food restaurants to be applied against future purchases, or we accumulate points for air travel.

The analogy that partners often collect emotional trading stamps is a good one. For example, you might be irritated because your partner left a piece of clothing lying on the floor. You say to yourself, "It's no big deal, I'll just pick it up myself and hang it in the closet." No big deal, of course, but an emotional trading stamp goes in the book. Sometime later you might find some dirty dishes left out on the counter and not put in the dishwasher. Again you think, "Oh well, no problem. I'll put them away." Another stamp is stuck in the book. And so it goes, until one day you discover some minor thing, such as your partner leaving on the lights. You go to your book and to your dismay you discover that it's full. Now the only option you have is to cash in. And, wow, do you *cash in!*

How many of you collect and save these kind of emotional trading stamps? Some of them might be labeled Guilt Stamps, Jealousy Stamps, Pity Stamps and Hostility Stamps. Maybe you can think of some favorite ones you collect.

The fact is that saving these stamps leads to a repression of your emotions, which when finally released can overwhelm yourself and your partner. Your partner may be totally stunned and wonder why the major reaction about such a minor irritant. If they are fortunate enough to catch on that this outburst is being triggered by a whole bunch of small offenses, they may have a chance to understand your anger. However, when the assault is intense it is difficult for anyone to remain calm and receptive.

It would be better not to wait until you have collected too many offences, but to deal with them in a timely and reasonable manner. Express your concern and share your difficulty in dealing with your

partner's behavior. Accept that what may be irritating to you is not at all uncomfortable for your partner. In fact, your partner may even find it difficult to stop the very behavior you find annoying.

Take the case of Susan and myself. Susan grew up in a home where lights were left on at all times, all over the house. It was actually a rule that lights were to be left on even throughout the night. In my house, the opposite was true. I was conditioned to turn off any light that was left on in any room that was not occupied. A light was certainly not allowed to stay on when we were sleeping. So here we were, with Susan turning on as many lights as she could, while I would be going around turning them off. We were both getting irritated. What saved us from a blow-up was our ability to talk it through, and express our personal feelings and preferences. It is no longer a major problem and can actually cause us to break out in laughter. One time I came home and found all the lights on. I didn't feel annoyed and simply began to turn off all the lights I didn't need, thinking, "I'll turn them back on before Susan comes back." Imagine my surprise when I heard a soft voice coming from a dark room, "Excuse me. I'm still in here."

Another answer that might prevent a "cashing in" incident would be that you each consider adjusting your behavior and diminishing the number of times you cause these little irritants. The first step is to become aware of the behavior that may be irritating to your partner. Before you think that everyone should be aware of the annoying things they do, think again. Too often, we do not see what other people see. I recall doing a number of "mock interviews" when I was working as a career counselor. These videotaped interviews were designed to help candidates improve their interviewing skills by reviewing their behavior. It never failed to surprise these candidates when I would stop the tape and ask them if they were aware of their distracting habits, like chewing on a pencil, breaking up a Styrofoam cup, or picking at clothing and body parts.

You may not consider any of the behaviors your partner finds annoying to be "such a big deal." However, it would be better for the health of your relationship if you accepted their opinion about their difficulty in dealing with them. Since they are no big deal, you might consider adjusting your behavior. And try to do what you can to stop yourself from collecting those emotional trading stamps.

The Blaming Game

The blaming game is perhaps the most popular game in the world. It requires a bit of extra attention here because too often we are not even aware when we are playing it. Some of us have grown up believing that when we feel wronged we should get even. We believe that justice will only be done when we make the wrongdoer suffer as much, or sometimes more, than we have. And so when we begin to experience unhappiness with our partner, we blame them and find ways to make their life just as miserable as is ours. I am not trying to challenge the justice systems in our world, but I would like to appeal to those people who blame their unhappiness on their partners.

Sometimes we grow up blaming almost everyone in our lives for our unhappiness. We blame our parents, our teachers, our friends or our brothers and sisters. Then we go out into the world and look for somebody to make us happy. We incorrectly assume that when we find the right person we will be fulfilled. We sometimes even envy other couples who appear to be happy and think, *They are only happy because they found the right partner*. We are like a cat that is chasing its tail. We believe that happiness is external, and forget to look inside ourselves for happiness. And so we are disappointed when our partner isn't making us happy. We continue our blaming game.

One of the basic truths I firmly believe in is that as adults we are totally responsible for our own joy. And as adults no one person can ever fill the hole in our soul. Only we can do that. Granted, we need relationships to remain healthy. However, we should not use them to unload our own unresolved anger.

Another truth is that you teach people how to treat you. If you recall in Chapter 1: Caring, I wrote about the games people play. In our desire to seek recognition, we often let people treat us in the way that they choose. When you are being put down or criticized by your partner, you need to take some responsibility for that behavior. When you stop letting your partner put you down, your partner will stop doing it. It's that simple, and yes, it is that hard. It takes courage and a good amount of self-confidence to stand up for your rights and say, "I'm no longer going to allow myself to be treated in this way." If your partner insults you, treats you disrespectfully or puts you down, you are well within your rights to tell them, "If you talk to me like that, I'm not going to stay here and listen."

Take responsibility for your own happiness, and stop blaming your partner for not giving you something that is not in their power to give.

Can I Take It Back?

Imagine for a moment that you are holding a tube of toothpaste in your hand. On the counter there is a glass into which you now squeeze all the toothpaste that is in the tube. Now that it is completely empty, your mission is to put it all back in the original tube. Mission impossible? Compare this to some of the things we say in the heat of the moment; we wish we could take the words back, but we can't. What do we do?

To say that you should never say anything you can't take back may be unrealistic. We all experience anger. Sometimes we may be angry and we don't even consciously realize it. It can be triggered in a flash and be gone just as quickly. Sadly, it is when we feel most vulnerable that we can sometimes experience a loss of control and lash

out. So what do loving partners do when one of them says something they wish they hadn't? The answer is "forgive."

As human beings we are imperfect and vulnerable. We do make mistakes. We make harsh statements and commit thoughtless acts. And yes, we need to do everything in our power to never hurt anyone. We also need to have the power and the strength to forgive. As Gerald G. Jampolsky says in his wonderful book *Forgiveness: The Greatest Healer of All,* "The happiest marriages are built on a foundation of forgiveness." He also makes it very clear that sometimes we become obsessed with seeking revenge and refusing to forget. That is when we remain a victim. Forgiveness means letting go of the past and moving forward. It is often the only way to achieve freedom and get past the hurt.

I have seen too many people who refused to forgive and did not even realize that the person who had hurt them was no longer in their lives. Yet, the anger and the hate they felt was still hurting them, eating away at their very soul. It was not only destroying them, it had destroyed their relationships.

Take Leslie's case. Leslie came for counseling because she was experiencing a lot of pain and suffering. Her doctor had prescribed some medication to help her with her physical symptoms. The doctor had also recommended that Leslie see a counselor to help relieve the emotional and psychological pain she was feeling. At the time, Leslie had been divorced for two and a half years. She was very bitter about the breakup of her 23-year marriage, and was very reluctant to let go of this painful past. When asked about her ability to forgive, she responded with, "Forgive him? Never! For what he did to me, I'll go to my grave hating him!" She was adamant about how the hurt and the pain she was feeling had been caused by her husband. She swore that she would never forget what had been done to her by "a spiteful and vindictive man." She said, "I'll never forget what he did. After all the years I devoted to that man!" She was not aware, however, of how she was allowing her suffering to continue. Each

time she reflected on the past, she would stir up her intense emotions, as if it were happening all over again. Her inability to forgive and forget prolonged her pain and suffering.

Eventually Leslie was able to see how her inability to forgive still made her a victim. In time, she freed herself from her self-imposed prison and moved on. She realized that the alternative would have been that her prediction, "I'll go to my grave hating him," may have come true sooner than she wished.

It took three years, but Leslie met another person she cared for, and who cared for her. She was able to love again. I will admit that moments like this bring joy to my life. I experience a wonderful feeling whenever I meet people who have the power to forgive and to free themselves to love again. It is wonderful when they are able to heal their wounds and rediscover the world. There have been other powerful moments in my life when I have seen people not only forgive but thank the people who hurt them. To admit that painful experiences had helped them develop into the strong individuals they are today takes great courage. However, these individuals bring joy back into their lives by their own actions.

Forgiveness is something I still personally struggle with. It is a work-in-progress. Forgiveness is a journey that I have been on for a long time and may never complete in my lifetime. However, I have always experienced a sense of liberation whenever I have been able to forgive the people who have hurt me, including myself.

Forgiving yourself can be one of the best things you can do to reclaim your self-confidence and self-worth. Take the case of Daniel. Daniel came for counseling because he blamed himself for all the fights in his relationship with Jenny. They had been married for only a year and the conflict has escalated to a point where Jenny had said she could not take it any more. For most of our sessions, Daniel came alone and would explore his tendency to "lose it" whenever he felt criticized by Jenny. During the sessions that Jenny attended, she revealed her history with an abusive father and expressed her fear that Daniel might become like him. It became clear that a pattern had set in during their short marriage where Jenny would express her fear and displeasure whenever Daniel got angry or upset. The problem was made worse by the fact that Daniel also severely criticized himself for getting angry. He admitted that he had lost his temper on several occasions but that he had, "never hit her, or laid a hand on her."

After a few sessions it became clear that Daniel had very high expectations of himself and was extremely self-critical. He had been beating himself up inside whenever he got angry. And each time he got angry he lost another piece of his self-confidence. His self-criticism had eaten away at him to the point where he doubted his ability to be a good companion. So whenever this inability to accept his imperfections was intensified by Jenny's criticism, it became too much for him and he lost control.

What eventually helped Daniel and Jenny was forgiveness. Mostly, it was Daniel's ability to forgive himself. He learned to accept himself and his flaws, and reclaim his self-worth. He gave himself permission to forget the past, to live in the present and look toward the future. He described his experience of self-forgiveness, "as if a giant weight has been lifted from me." The fights diminished and the healing began.

Forgiveness is such a compelling topic and since I cannot do justice to it in this book, I suggest you and your partner explore the healing power of this loving act together. I will end this section with David Augsburger's powerful message:

"Forgiveness is letting what was, be gone; What will be, come; What is now, be."

Write It Down

During my training, I was taught a technique that has helped many of my clients as well as myself. It is an excellent approach to help

you sort out your feelings of anger. All that is required is that you sit down and write out your thoughts on paper.

The following 10 points are important to remember if you are going to use this approach:

1. Don't wait until you have cooled down. Write out your thoughts while you are still experiencing your reaction. It is important that you let yourself feel the emotion in the moment, and not try simply to imagine what you felt like.
2. Don't worry about grammar, spelling or neatness. This is for you only to read.
3. Do let it flow. Write whatever comes into your awareness. You do not need to edit or delete anything. Just keep writing.
4. Do use a pencil, preferably a soft one. Using a computer and typing out your ideas may be too artificial. The act of physically writing, and feeling the pencil flow over the page, is very therapeutic.
5. Do sit somewhere comfortable and private. Pick a favorite place where you will not be interrupted.
6. Do write quickly and not for a long period of time. After about ten or fifteen minutes, you will have uncovered and identified some hidden feelings.
7. Do describe what happened. Write down how you reacted and what triggered your reaction.
8. Do describe what you are feeling, not just what you are thinking. Get in touch with your emotional reaction. This is not a technique to be used as a way to avoid your feelings.
9. Do explore what this situation reminds you of. Without censoring, write down anything that comes into your awareness.
10. Do reflect on what you have written. When you have finished writing, and the intensity of your emotion begins to subside, review what thoughts, images and feelings came to your awareness.

In the case of Brent and Crystal, this technique resolved what could have been a real crisis. It all happened over a plant. The plant was actually a small tree that Brent had bought during the first year of their marriage. He was quite fond of his little tree and always made sure it was watered, fed and trimmed.

During the eight years of their marriage, Crystal and Brent had moved three times, and each time his little tree had survived these moves. Unfortunately, after the last move, Brent had inadvertently placed his tree under an air-conditioning vent. Within a few days, the leaves started to turn brown and began to drop. No matter what he did, the leaves kept falling. He even called some specialists to ask what could be done, to no avail. His battle to save his beloved tree was being lost. After a month, there were few leaves left on the branches.

One day Brent was immersed in some paperwork when Crystal called him from the other room: "Come see what I did, Brent." Because Brent was struggling to finish a report, he was a bit reluctant to get up and walk over. When he arrived he was not prepared for what he saw. He described it as follows: "I simply froze. There in front of me was Crystal with trimming shears, and she had cut all the branches off my tree. All that was left was the trunk, and very little of that. I recall she actually looked pleased, while the only thing I could feel was the anger welling up inside. I remember thinking, *How could she do this? After all my work to try and save that tree, and she's destroyed it. How could she?* I was so angry I couldn't speak. All I remember saying was that I needed to go away for a bit and that we'd talk about it later."

Brent went back to the room where he had been working and began to write down his feelings. He described writing whatever came to his awareness, of being full of anger and mad at Crystal for doing something so thoughtless. He was also mad at himself for being so stupid as to place his sensitive benjamina under the air-conditioning vent. He knew that act had actually killed the tree.

Eventually he started to reflect on Crystal's motives. He knew her as a caring person, and he couldn't recall a time when she had knowingly wanted to hurt anyone. After about fifteen minutes, he came back to talk to her. The only question he could ask was, "Why?" With tears in her eyes, Crystal said, "I didn't mean to hurt you. I actually wanted to help. I knew you weren't going to give up trying to save your tree. But I also saw you getting stressed and angry with yourself for not being able to fix it. I didn't want you to be upset any more, so I decided to make the decision for you. I did what had to be done. I'm sorry you feel hurt."

I'm sure as you read this case example you can imagine how this event could have escalated into a bitter fight where both partners might have blamed each other for the pain and suffering that was caused. Instead, the strength of their feelings for each other, and their ability to wait, reflect and understand the other's perception, brought healing to this event instead of additional pain. Their ability to explore and resolve this potentially destructive event showed not only the strength of their conflict resolution skills, it revealed the real health of their relationship.

There are times when it is necessary for you to go away and reflect on what has happened—times when you are so upset, it might be harmful to stay and discuss the issue with your partner. Remember, you cannot be reasonable when you are experiencing the stress of a strong emotion like anger. These are the times when writing down your thoughts and feelings will help you to analyze your experience and learn from it. Each time you learn how your own emotions can be triggered by your perception of the event, you will begin to take more responsibility for your reactions. Your tendency to blame, or put the responsibility for your feelings on your partner, will diminish. You will discover those hidden feelings that have everything to do with you, and nothing to do with your partner.

Talk It Out

Another powerful way to discover how you upset yourself is to talk it out with a good listener. The experience will be most powerful if the good listener happens to be your intimate partner. Unfortunately, for the listener, it is extremely difficult to be a good listener when you are personally involved in the problem you are trying to solve. And therein lies part of the problem. The very fact that you are trying to solve your partner's problem, is a problem. When you are doing that, you are concentrating more on how to respond, and what solution to present, than you are engaged in just listening.

I will admit right here that this is a skill that sometimes eludes me when I'm listening to Susan. Oh sure, I can be a good listener when I'm working with my clients. After all, I'm not personally involved in their suffering. However, when it comes to my intimate partner, I still find it hard at times to stop myself from trying to present a solution...especially when she says I'm the problem. I also find that my tendency to want to help can interfere when I jump in and try to make her feel better, when all she really wants and needs is for me to listen.

So what's the answer? Well, what sometimes works is when Susan tells me, "Please! Just listen!" What works better, of course, is when I remember to do that on my own. Over time I have learned to recognize my typical behaviors that show I'm not really listening. See if you recognize any of these behaviors as your own:

1. You try to reassure your partner that everything is going to be fine before they have a chance to finish expressing their feelings.
2. You begin to interpret what your partner is feeling before they do so themselves.
3. You interrupt your partner with your own agenda and start talking about how *you* feel.

4. You get so focused on the problem your partner started presenting, that you don't realize they're testing you to see if you'll listen to what they really want to say.
5. *And the winner*: You play the role of psychotherapist.

The reason I say number five is the winner, is because it is the behavior of which I have been most guilty. Ever since I met Susan I have had to stop myself from taking on this role. Originally, during the first years of our relationship, I really believed that I was helping. I could not accept her anger at me for trying to help. I did not realize that I was crossing the line. In this case, crossing the line meant psychoanalyzing her behavior and telling her what she "should" do. A word of warning might be useful here: All of the suggestions presented in this book are for your personal use. As stated so insightfully by James Creighton in his book *How Loving Couples Fight*, "As our knowledge of human behavior increases, it becomes a real temptation to analyze our friends, loved ones, and co-workers. The only problem is that we are not usually invited to be their psychotherapists."

The more aware you become of these behaviors, the more quickly you can stop yourself. However, it is important to accept that there will be times when you are both so upset with each other that it is virtually impossible for either one of you to let the other one talk it out. And even if you can, your efforts may not be appreciated. As Susan has thankfully pointed out to me, there is nothing more irritating than for me to show my superiority in active listening when we are in the middle of an emotional disagreement.

There are, of course, other behaviors that will stop your partner from sharing their concerns and attempting to resolve a conflict with you. See if you recognize any of the following:

1. You say, "I know what you're going to say," as soon as your partner starts talking.
2. You claim to have a headache, or that you're getting too upset.

3. You counterattack by telling your partner what they did wrong.
4. You claim ignorance and pretend you don't understand what their problem is.
5. You make your partner responsible for the problem, suggesting you don't have that problem.
6. You turn it into an intellectual discussion, ignoring the real feelings your partner is experiencing.
7. You pretend not to be concerned, acting as if their issue is unimportant or even unworthy of your time.

Any of these behaviors would seriously impede resolving any differences between you. If you genuinely want to hear your partner's concerns, it is important to remember that you are equals. Go easy on the judgments and on presenting solutions.

Resolving a conflict between partners happens more quickly when you both feel equal.

When All Else Fails

No matter how hard you try, no matter how much you care, there will be times when you simply have to agree to disagree. Accept that you are both entitled to your own points of view. You may both feel that your position is justified. When that happens, you may not want to "give in." There are times when it is best to "hold your ground." **A loving partner will never force you to give up your values.**

However, if you start to experience resentment, and you are not able to resolve a conflict to your satisfaction, you may want to consider help from an outside source. Accept that sometimes love is not enough. Sometimes you may need an objective person who can help you determine your difficulty in solving the problem.

Seek out a person you both trust, one who is neutral and will not

take sides. Sometimes it is best to work with a trained professional who is able to focus on you and your relationship while remaining neutral. Counselors, psychotherapists, psychologists, social workers, psychiatrists, mediators, ministers, rabbis, and pastoral counselors are all potential resources. Remember to choose someone whom you both trust and are comfortable with, is trained in conflict resolution and who will remain neutral.

Conflict is a normal part of a healthy relationship. The key is that both partners feel good about the resolution.

What Is Your Conflict IQ? (Me)

The first step to improving any skill is to determine how skilled you are. You need to have a measurement of your ability before you can develop a strategy on how and what to improve. After reading each question, give yourself a score of one to five. When you finish, add up your score and review the results with your partner.

Never		Sometimes		Always
1	2	3	4	5

Do you take responsibility for the outcome of your conflicts? _____

Do you accept responsibility for your own reaction, rather than blame your partner? _____

Do you find it easy to say "I'm sorry" or "I was wrong"? _____

Do you work to achieve a resolution that satisfies both of your needs and interests (win-win)? _____

Do you deal with minor irritants before they pile up? _____

Are you able to put yourself in your partner's place? _____

Do you explore alternatives, rather than offer a solution? _____

Do you know your partner's "hot buttons" and stay away from pushing them? _____

Do you stick to the issue without dragging in old wounds from the past or bringing up new topics? _____

Do you choose a time and place that is acceptable to both of you? _____

Are you aware of your own "hot buttons"? _____

Do you refrain from making threats and ultimatums? _____

Total Points

Enter your total score here: ______

What Is Your Conflict IQ? (Partner)

After reading each question, give yourself a score of one to five. When you finish, add up your score and review the results with your partner.

Never		**Sometimes**		**Always**
1	**2**	**3**	**4**	**5**

Do you take responsibility for the outcome of your conflicts? _____

Do you accept responsibility for your own reaction, rather than blame your partner? _____

Do you find it easy to say "I'm sorry" or "I was wrong"? _____

Do you work to achieve a resolution that satisfies both of your needs and interests (win-win)? _____

Do you deal with minor irritants before they pile up? _____

Are you able to put yourself in your partner's place? _____

Do you explore alternatives, rather than offer a solution? _____
Do you know your partner's "hot buttons"
and stay away from pushing them? _____
Do you stick to the issue without dragging in old
wounds from the past or bringing up new topics? _____
Do you choose a time and place that is acceptable
to both of you? _____
Are you aware of your own "hot buttons"? _____
Do you refrain from making threats and ultimatums? _____

Total Points

Enter your total score here: _____

Results

40 or above: Congratulations. You practice good conflict resolution skills. You are also contributing to a greater closeness and secure bond in your loving relationship. Continue to improve your skills and you will resolve the hurts and differences that arise between you and your partner. You will also improve your own emotional and physical health.

Below 40: Discuss with your partner what conflict resolution skills you do well. Find out what other skills would be appreciated, and determine which of these you would be willing to practice and improve. Every time you solve a problem you are contributing to a closer and more secure relationship. Go for the win-win solution.

Add your own: There may be other conflict resolution skills that you practice that are not described in the previous exercise. Discuss these with your partner and decide whether or not they qualify. Any skill that resolves your disagreements helps build a stronger relationship. Feel free to list these skills on the following page. Score these skills and add the points to your results.

My own conflict resolution skills:

My partner's conflict resolution skills:

Reflect

Reflect on your disagreements. Is there a pattern? What do you do when you reach an impasse and you cannot seem to resolve your disagreement? Do you agree to discuss it at another time? Do you treat each other with respect, and as equal partners? Think about your relationship and how it is affected by the way you deal with conflict.

What do you need to do to handle your conflicts better? Are you taking responsibility for the way you fight? Jot down a few notes about what you can do, and what you want to accomplish.

Me

My Partner

A Beautiful Balance

Sometimes you start a fight and I try to resolve it, and sometimes I start a fight and you try to resolve it, and sometimes we both try to resolve it no matter who starts it. It is all a beautiful balance. It is a loving relationship when two people respect each other, have developed the ability to fight fair, and work together to resolve their disagreements.

Make a commitment to continue to improve your conflict resolution skills. List what you will do in the space below. Work together as loving partners to develop your list. Choose what you consider to be the most important skill you need to improve to build a healthy relationship. Transfer this choice to your self-contract at the end of this book.

Me

____

____

____

____

____

____

____

____

My Partner

____

____

____

____

____

____

____

____

Creativity

The best person to have a love affair with is your loving partner.

The Fun Stuff

"I miss the playfulness and the unexpected."

Many couples have become locked into familiar routines. They wish they could recapture those moments when as a young couple they would react with joy and anticipation when their partner walked into the room. They long for the days when they were spontaneous and enthusiastic about seemingly everything. Life has become predictable and boring. They wonder where the romance has gone.

If you are one of these couples you will be pleased to discover that you do not have to find a time machine to whisk you back to those more exciting times. The person who can become completely absorbed in the moment and find joy in the simplest things exists inside of you. You can recapture those delightful times and liven up your relationship. You can keep it fresh and fun. All it takes is some creativity.

Creativity involves trusting yourself and your own intuition. That means letting go of your familiar thinking and predictable routines and allowing the magic back into your life. Follow your heart and allow it to lead you to a more spontaneous and joyful self. Trust that inner voice to know what changes you need to make in your life. Remember, the very best relationships flourish on growth and change.

Creativity also means taking a risk and doing the unexpected. Be willing to do something that you have never done before. You will never be bored if you are willing to experiment and include variety in your relationship. It doesn't matter if you have been together for just one year or more than 25 years. Bring back the elements of surprise and playfulness to your relationship. Remember when you're in a rut that the only way out is to do something new and different. It doesn't matter how silly it may seem as long as it's fun. Spice up your life and bring the romance back. If you don't, you may find yourself or your partner longing for another relationship.

Create Your Own Private Space

One of the basic things that many couples forget about is how they are affected by their surroundings. When it comes to romance, atmosphere can be one of the most important factors. Think about how you feel and how you behave when you are walking on a moonlit beach during a pleasant summer night. You are likely holding hands and feeling close to your partner. Now imagine that you are walking along on a busy sidewalk during rush hour. You may be holding hands, but it's probably motivated more by a desire for protection than for romance.

Now look around your bedroom. What do you see? Are there workbooks and papers scattered all around? Do you see a comput-

er? Is there a briefcase or other work-related items on the dresser, or next to the bed? If you find any of these items, I suggest you remember the following: the bedroom is for the two "S"s, and they stand for "sex" and "sleep." One of them is *not* "study."

The bedroom is one of the most important rooms in the house when it comes to an intimate relationship. It is the one room where you and your partner spend most of your time together. It is also a place where you are influenced by your surroundings every time you lay your head on the pillow. Bedrooms are meant to be private places where you experience pleasure and peace. Not stress and chaos. It is your private chamber. So get rid of the clutter, including the kids' toys. Remove that exercise machine with the sweaty towels hanging from it. If you can't put it anywhere else, at least screen it off. In other words, remove anything that might dampen the flame of romance.

Susan and I recently had to do just that. We had received a picture of our three lovely grandchildren. We liked it so much we immediately put in on the wall in our bedroom, thinking we would be able to see their smiling faces every time we awoke. The problem, however, did not take long to become apparent. As I walked around the room I could see their young eyes follow me wherever I went. It didn't matter where I was in the room, I could see them looking at me. The picture is now in our family room where it belongs, and has been replaced with a picture of the two of us enjoying ourselves on a beach.

Together with your partner, decorate your bedroom according to your romantic taste. Create an atmosphere that will ignite feelings of love. One of you may like frills, the other a vibrant color. Discuss and choose the combination that appeals to you both. Make it the kind of room you look forward to entering and one that creates the feelings you desire.

So, go ahead and create the atmosphere you want. Get rid of the clutter and non-essentials. Be creative, even with those special items you might need during a spontaneous and loving moment. Put them where you can easily reach them. Nothing can break the mood more quickly then having to stop the action to look for one of those "essentials."

Look at Yourself

That's right, looks count. Look at yourself in the mirror and see if your reflection would spark some romantic feelings in your partner. Will your partner's eyes light up with joy and anticipation when you walk into the bedroom? Or will you receive the kind of reaction where their eyes are tightly shut, pretending to be asleep? Are you wearing those sweats that were hanging on the exercise machine, or did you change into a comfortable and appealing outfit?

The feel and smell of your skin is another important consideration. The way a person smells and feels can be a huge attraction. It can also be an instant turnoff. I suggest you go for the former and find out what your partner likes. Also remember to praise your partner if they have put in the effort to make themselves appealing. Remember, nothing reinforces the behavior you want as much as a positive and appropriate compliment.

Your physical appearance is perhaps the easiest to adjust, and yet the most neglected part of creating the right atmosphere. In many cases, it only involves personal hygiene and good grooming. And let's face it, you may already be doing it for your work environment, so why not put in the same amount of effort taking care of your appearance for your partner? Even the simple and refreshing act of brushing your teeth and taking a shower or a relaxing bath, can have a positive effect on both your partner and yourself. At the very least you will both feel more comfortable about being close to each other. The best outcome would be if both of you were to physically touch each other before you go to sleep. Remember our physical need to be touched, and how healthy it is for us to receive regular skin contact?

Well, here's your chance to do something really healthy for each other.

If you want to rid yourself of the pressures and stress of your daily activities, a pleasing back rub or a long and tender hug will be very healing. Take a good long look at yourself and decide whether or not you like what you see.

Go ahead and make yourself "huggable." It is a very healthy thing to do for yourself and your relationship.

The First Impression

What you do and say during the first few minutes when you meet and greet your partner is very important. It can set the tone for the rest of the day or evening. Using a nurturing and supportive approach in your greeting will result in a better outcome. It may also be important for you to change your regular routine. Too often we are busily involved in some activity and we ignore our partner when they walk through the door. Or we are the one who walks in and immediately gets busy sorting out the mail, or checking the e-mail. We haven't seen each other for hours and what do we do? We pay more attention to "things" than we do to the living and breathing person with whom we share our lives. When we do that, we create a distance that isolates us from our partner. And then we wonder why we feel ignored and alone.

Whenever you feel ignored and alone it is important to remember that you are responsible for your own happiness. You have taught your partner how to treat you. So take the initiative, change your predictable routine and do something unexpected. Instead of ignoring your partner and asking the usual superficial, "How was your day?" while still continuing your activity, you might want to try the following three steps:

1. Stop whatever it is you're doing and make eye contact with your partner.
2. Give your partner a long passionate kiss. Not just a peck on the cheek, or a quick brush on the lips, but a slow, lingering kiss.
3. Concentrate on each other, and take turns sharing your day.

The total amount of time may be no more than a few minutes, but it will create an atmosphere of closeness that may last for the entire evening. Invest a little bit of your time; the return will be well worth it.

What you are doing in those first few minutes is creating a good first impression. And we all know the saying, "You never have a second chance to make a good first impression." Those first few precious minutes are all it takes to create the mood and the atmosphere. So take responsibility for how you are treated by your partner and turn that response into one that you will both savor and enjoy. Imagine the results if you both were to use this creative first impression.

Doing It Together

Do you share a lot of the same interests? If you are like many couples, the answer is "no." You may have many similar values; however, the activities you are interested in are often very different from your partner's. For a relationship to be healthy, you do not need to share all your interests. However, having some common interests, and looking for ways to increase those shared activities, can make your relationship even healthier.

The following is an exercise I have encouraged couples to complete in order to increase the activities they share. The feedback received from the couples that completed this exercise has been very positive, and that has surprised many of them. The biggest surprise was that

they did not realize that certain activities they had been avoiding were, in fact, quite pleasant, and in some cases downright fun.

Here's what you both do. Each of you make a list of the leisure activities you enjoy. Do not take into consideration your partner's likes or dislikes. This is strictly your own personal list. Your list can include anything you like, whether it involves a sport, a hobby, going to a play or movie, reading certain books, taking a course, arranging flowers, riding a bike, going for a walk, shopping, keeping an album, watching television or surfing the Internet. Include anything that you are currently involved in, as well as things you would like to do. Put on your list whatever you are interested in, no matter what it is. The only activities *not* to include are any that are related to earning an income.

Once you have completed your list:

1. Decide which of these activities are your very favorites, and number your choices in order of priority.
2. Select 10 activities you really enjoy, and plan to do in the future, and transfer these onto the following chart.
3. Give the completed list to your partner for review.
4. Repeat the process with your partner making a list.
5. From your partner's list you may remove up to seven activities that *you* would not enjoy doing. This leaves at least three activities that you could share with your partner.

Shared Activities (Me)

1. ______________________________
2. ______________________________
3. ______________________________
4. ______________________________
5. ______________________________

6. ______________________________
7. ______________________________
8. ______________________________
9. ______________________________
10. ______________________________

Shared Activities (Partner)

1. ______________________________
2. ______________________________
3. ______________________________
4. ______________________________
5. ______________________________
6. ______________________________
7. ______________________________
8. ______________________________
9. ______________________________
10. ______________________________

Since each of you will have at least three activities remaining on your original list, you now have to decide how and when you will share these activities. The beauty of this exercise is that you have agreed on at least three activities from each list that you will share with each other. I have seen this result in a couple sharing six activities when previously they had not shared any. Also, in case you are concerned that you lose something in this deal, you can still engage in the activities that your partner removed from your list. You may choose to do these alone or with others.

This creative way of finding things to do together has worked really well, not only for many of my clients, but also for Susan and myself. After doing this exercise, and removing seven items from Susan's list, I was still left with one that I really did not look forward to doing.

However, I had agreed to at least try it. It was "going to a flea market." Susan had been enjoying this activity for some time, and would come home all excited about the bargains she had found. At the time, I had begun what would be a five-year project constructing an experimental, homebuilt aircraft. To my pleasant surprise, I discovered a wealth of tools and supplies at these flea markets that could be used in my building project. There were even times when I dragged Susan along because I needed something.

As for some of the other things removed from my list, I was still able to participate in these. For example, Susan is not a fan of being in the ocean. So whenever we go to warmer climates, she goes shopping while I go scuba diving for a few hours. We then meet for lunch and share our adventures.

Can't Think of Anything to Do Together?

To help your creative juices, just review the following list of 30 potential things to do:

1. Cook an unusual dish.
2. Ride your bikes in the countryside.
3. Join a health club.
4. Visit a museum.
5. Go for a long walk.
6. Eat at a new restaurant.
7. Visit a library.
8. Review a newspaper or magazine.
9. Go to a movie.
10. Learn a new hobby or craft.
11. Visit a zoo.
12. Learn or participate in a new sport.
13. Take a special interest course.
14. Volunteer at your local community center.

15. Go to a place of worship.
16. Visit an amusement park.
17. Start a collection.
18. Decorate your home.
19. Go swimming.
20. Visit friends.
21. Work on a political campaign.
22. Take dancing lessons.
23. Go on a picnic.
24. Attend a concert.
25. Play on the computer.
26. Go to the ballet.
27. Enter a contest.
28. Go camping.
29. Go on a canoe trip.
30. Watch the sunset.

The list is endless…

Where's the Sizzle?

Do you suffer from sexual boredom? Are you trying to have perfect sex? Do you use sex as a control weapon? Do you sometimes believe that you would be happier if sex were eliminated altogether from your relationship? If you answered "yes" to any of these questions, then take heart, help is as close as your intimate partner. The key to recapturing a satisfying sexual relationship is good communication and willingness for both partners to explore and work together on their sexual problems.

The first step to fixing any problem is to recognize that there is a problem. When it comes to sex, it is important to understand that it is a requirement for a healthy relationship. If you recall, all the

studies and research presented earlier prove that we need to be touched. Our survival and well-being depends on physical contact. Sexual contact between loving partners is not only one of the best ways to maintain your physical and emotional health, it will also extend your lifespan.

Sexual contact is also a great stress reliever. There are three activities that produce positive chemical reactions in our bodies which act as an antidote to stress-produced adrenaline. They are: exercise, laughter and a good roll in the hay. The activity of sex produces a peak pleasure experience that triggers the body's endocrine system. And that's great news, because in today's stressful world, we depend on our body's ability to deal with these attacks against our immune system.

It is also important to accept that sex is not always about intercourse. The most satisfying, and sometimes the most erotic, sex can be experienced before you get to the climax. Many couples have learned that the very act of teasing can create a heightening of their sexual feelings. It is not about finishing, it is better to prolong the pleasure. Even the simple act of being flirtatious and creating a feeling of anticipation can be incredibly erotic.

If you find yourself withholding sex from your partner, you may need to look at the control issues in your relationship. Perhaps you feel that your partner is controlling you and that the only way you can regain some power is to use sex as a weapon. If that is the case you need to realize that withholding sex is a very destructive weapon that is harmful to both you and your partner. Stop using sex as a battleground, and work at establishing a sense of equality in your relationship.

For many couples, sex is the bond that keeps their partnership together. They understand that one of the best ways of preventing affairs is to have a great intimate relationship. They also accept that great sex is not about quantity, it is about quality. Don't be fooled by what you see in the movies. Good sex is not about breaking records and seeing how long you can last, it is about pleasuring each other and experiencing sexual satisfaction.

What I hear mostly from my clients is they would like a longer warm-up time in their sexual activity. That means they would find it more enjoyable if their partner would concentrate more on staying in the moment and not rush to get to the climax. Make it an act of love and be aware of how you make each other feel, rather than how often you "do it." There is no pressure to have great sex every time. It is not a competition, and you can always do it again another time.

There is already enough pressure in our lives. Yet sometimes we find ourselves demanding that our partner have sex with us, even when they are not in the mood. Don't just demand it and expect your partner to be responsive to that kind of approach. Putting more pressure on your partner is not going to get you what you want. It just doesn't work. What may work is finding out what puts your partner in the mood, and taking responsibility for making that happen. Be creative and explore the various ways you can trigger the kind of response you desire. Don't be demanding of yourself either.

Putting pressure on yourself is a surefire way to diminish the pleasure for both of you.

There are three basic rules for a satisfying sexual relationship:

1. Understand your own, as well as your partner's, sexuality and find out what you both enjoy.
2. Do whatever brings you both joy and pleasure, and stop doing anything that is uncomfortable or unsatisfying.
3. If you practice rules number one and two, there are no other rules.

It may surprise some of you to know that many older couples say their sex lives have improved with age. They claim that they experienced the best sex long after many people assume sex is supposed to be over. This revelation does not mean that good sex is only attainable by older couples. In fact, great sex can be experienced by intimate couples of all ages. The main factors are love, trust, respect and a special closeness that can only be achieved by partners practicing the first three.

One of the best ways to spark up your sex life and bring the romance back into your relationship is to go on a date. In case you are wondering if I practice what I preach, let me present the following personal example: A short time ago I was getting myself stressed about meeting the deadline for this manuscript. I had been struggling with one chapter that just didn't seem to flow, when the phone rang. I reluctantly picked it up, thinking, "I don't really need an interruption right now." My thinking quickly changed, however, as soon as I heard the soothing and rather sexy tone of Susan's voice asking me out on a date. She was calling on her cell phone from somewhere inside the house. I still remember her words, "Hey, handsome. This is your partner speaking (it took me a second to realize she was referring to our business partnership). How would you like a sexy date with your VP?" I think at that point I just stammered. Imagine me being at a loss for words. She then invited me to meet her "downstairs in an hour for a nice glass of wine and some intimate communication." Before I knew it, I was in the shower anticipating our date.

The stress I was experiencing just minutes before she phoned was quickly disappearing. I put on my sexiest (according to Susan) shirt and made myself comfortable downstairs. The excitement seemed to build inside of me. Then she appeared, dressed in a very classy business outfit, but with some buttons strategically left undone. I tell you, even now as I am writing this, the memory of that evening brings back some incredible feelings. If you don't mind, I'll just leave those to your imagination.

I consider myself extremely fortunate to have a loving partner who is not afraid to initiate or respond to a spontaneous, erotic moment. Our relationship has greatly benefited from our ability to read each other and choose an appropriate time to create one of these memorable moments.

You can do the same. You can find the sizzle and rekindle your love affair with your partner. All it takes is spontaneity and creativity. Explore and discover what lights the fire for each of you. Use whatever works. For more ideas, you may find it helpful to read the section called *50 Ways to Keep Your Lover*, at the end of this chapter.

The Valentine's Day Challenge

Just this past Valentine's Day, when I was giving a speech to a large group of couples, I asked them to share with the group their best romantic experience, something they considered different, unique and loving. I told them that we would choose the best three examples and include the stories and their names in this book. Surprisingly, not many couples submitted descriptions for our review. Some of the couples I spoke with after the presentation revealed that they had what they considered an enduring relationship that had become somewhat routine. They were content, yet they longed for some spontaneity and playfulness.

The following examples include surprise, playfulness and romance. We did not rate them as to which one was the "best."

The Surprise:

One cold, Friday afternoon in February, Dave picked me up at work. We had spoken that afternoon and he said he was taking me out for supper. So off we went, Dave behind the wheel, driving

along, with me not knowing where we were going. Some time passed before I realized we were leaving the city and were traveling along a main highway heading south. By this time I assumed we were driving to another city for dinner. Time passed and I was getting more confused. Dave seemed to be heading towards the Canadian/US border. As we approached the border Dave leaned over and asked me to play along with what he was going to tell the border guard. We were asked the usual questions about citizenship, where we lived and of course, "Where are you going, and for how long?" Dave answers, "We are going to Florida on a two-week holiday." Needless to say, I was shocked. Moving through the border I told Dave he should not have lied because we could get in trouble. He just smiled and told me to look in the glove compartment. In it I found a letter from some friends we knew in Florida. It read: "It is true. You are on your way to see us. Enjoy the trip."

My very romantic husband had made all the arrangements. He had even booked off two weeks holidays for me, packed my suitcases (I was told that if he forgot anything I could buy it once we got there), reserved the hotel rooms, and hired a house and pet sitter. It was a fantastic trip and we had a fabulous time.

Lyne and Dave Hallett

The Five Senses:

It was the most romantic birthday celebration that we had shared together. My husband treated my five senses. Each gift was a feeling and thought embodied in love. Howard took a great deal of time and care when choosing the gifts. The feelings of love were very apparent.

For the sense of smell he bought me fressias—my favorite flower. My sense of taste was overwhelmed by chocolate-covered ginger—my idea of an "oral orgasmic experience," the ultimate aphrodisiac. Next was the sense of sight. He rented the video *Ghost*, the best two-box-of-Kleenex movie. I cried while he was holding me in his arms.

The fourth sense of hearing was satisfied by a CD he gave me. On it was the music played at our wedding, including the song "Fly Me to the Moon." The fifth and last sense was the sense of touch. With this gift my husband played a little trick on me. He gave me a set of satin sheets for our waterbed. Howard then said they were a gift for the bed and that my real gift was still to come.

He then took me out for dinner, and while in the car he told me to open the glove compartment. Inside I found a small box with a red bow on top. I opened the box to find beautiful pearl earrings, surrounded by double hearts. This gift really touched my soul. I always smile, inside and out, when I wear my birthday earrings—which, by the way, is often.

Michelle and Howard Rosenblum

The Trip to Paradise:

This past Valentine's Day I was freshening up after work when Colin corralled me and encouraged me to go into our bedroom. He asked me to "stay there till I tell you to come out." After several minutes I started to hear Caribbean sounds drifting through the door. Not long after, he opened the door and escorted me to the living room, dressed in tropical clothing. What I saw when we arrived melted my heart. Colin had sprinkled the entire room with rose petals. Candles were burning all over the place. On the floor, in front of the fireplace, he had placed some blankets and comfortable cushions, while the sound of ocean waves and tropical music played in the background. Colin also served a wonderful meal, complimented with my favorite wine, right there on his makeshift beach. My loving partner had truly brought paradise into our home. It was one of the most romantic evenings of our relationship.

The previous Valentine's Day, Colin had also shown his romantic flair and a preference for rose petals. When I arrived home he asked me to go on a treasure hunt. My only instructions were to "follow

the petals. They will lead to your treasure." After a series of twists and turns throughout our house, the rose petals took me to a gift-wrapped box. Inside were a beautiful pendant and pair of earrings. I was so moved by his gift, yet it is because of the rose petals that I remember it so well. It was that little touch of creativity that really made it romantic and special. Every time I wear that gift I think about that night, and how special it was.

Cyndi Edwards and Colin Trethewey

Sometimes it truly is "the thought that counts." For Colin, it only took twelve dollars worth of roses to create a memory that will last a lifetime. This is a great example of the power of creativity. [I invite you to submit your personal romantic experience that I may share with an audience or publish in a future book.]

50 Ways to Keep Your Lover

Is your relationship as romantic today as it was when you and your partner first met? If your answer is "not really"—you could benefit from choosing one of the following romantic suggestions:

1. Say "I love you" everyday.
2. Rediscover those long, passionate kisses.
3. Set some time aside and go on a special date.
4. Make it a habit to cuddle and hold each other tenderly.
5. At the next social function, flirt with your partner.
6. Compliment your partner in front of others. Never use sarcasm or put them down.
7. Make a truly equal partnership. Share everything.
8. Always make a special effort for birthdays, anniversaries or any special day.

9. Be happy and laugh together. It sets the stage for an upbeat night.
10. Send flowers or give a gift for no occasion.
11. Renew your vows.
12. Put your partner before all others and they will be with you till the end.
13. Take time to share your deepest feelings and what is in your heart.
14. Hold hands when walking together in public.
15. Schedule time for sex. Go to bed one hour earlier or set your alarm one hour earlier.
16. Compliment each other regularly; "gorgeous" or "handsome" may be well received.
17. Cuddle up when you're watching TV.
18. E-mail "I love you."
19. Touch each other a lot, even in public.
20. Stay in bed together on weekends an extra hour and just "spoon" or "snuggle."
21. Whisper something sexy to your partner while in public.
22. Go for a romantic drive and find a place to watch the sunset.
23. Hide a love note in your partner's briefcase or luggage.
24. Make each other a priority. Plan an erotic evening and anticipate the time.
25. Leave a sexy message for your partner on the answering machine.
26. Dedicate a song on the radio.
27. Have a special photo framed from your last romantic getaway and display it at work.
28. Tell your partner how much they still turn you on.
29. Go for a walk in the rain.
30. Pack a picnic for two, and go to your favorite place.

31. Read this book together and put the 7 "C"s into practice.
32. Don't wait to go for a romantic dinner, take time to meet at lunch.
33. Make out some "love coupons" for your partner to redeem.
34. Take a massage course together and practice on each other.
35. Pretend you're strangers and meet at a trendy bar to pick each other up.
36. Meet at a hotel and have a "nooner."
37. Dress up. Spend a night at home with a favorite bottle of wine and music, and slow dance.
38. Have fun. Don't just have sex in your bedroom. Be creative and try all the rooms in the house.
39. Leave a trail of sexy notes, starting at the front door, with clues for where to find you.
40. Have a spa night and pamper each other.
41. Strip your partner, or play strip poker.
42. Cook a romantic dinner together, and serve it in the nude.
43. Watch an erotic video, made specifically for couples, together.
44. Explore each other's body and discover the "sensual spots."
45. Don't go for the finish. Enjoy the journey.
46. Explore and share your secret fantasy.
47. Visit a love shop together and pick out some "special toys."
48. Whatever competitive sport or game you play together, winner gets to choose the reward for the evening.
49. Be the first to initiate. Don't wait for your partner.
50. Add your own 50 Ways to Keep Your Lover.

Reflect

Reflect on how creative you are. Can you remember a time when you were spontaneous and enthusiastic about seemingly everything? Think about your relationship and how your ability to be spontaneous and creative affects your relationship and yourself. Are you able to let go of your familiar thinking and predictable routines?

What do you need to do to be more creative? Are you taking responsibility for the amount of fun and spontaneity in your relationship? Jot down a few notes about what you can do, and what you want to accomplish.

Me

My Partner

A Beautiful Balance

Sometimes you are creative, and sometimes I am creative, and sometimes we are both creative. It is all a beautiful balance. It is a loving relationship where two people trust each other enough to be spontaneous, and let the magic back into their lives.

Make a commitment to be a more creative partner. List what you will do in the space below. Work together as loving partners to develop your list. Choose what you consider to be the most creative thing you could do to bring joy and pleasure to your relationship. Transfer this choice to your self-contract at the end of this book.

Me

My Partner

Commitment

The trick in life isn't in getting what you want. It's wanting it after you get it.

Katharine Hepburn (from the movie *Love Affair)*

The Contract

"Why are some promises easier to keep than others?"

How many promises have you made that you didn't keep? If your answer is "a few," then perhaps it is time to look at what you can do to keep your promises and commitments. Let's start with the basics. *Webster's Dictionary* defines commitment as, "an agreement or pledge to do something in the future." In this case, you agree and pledge to practice some of the things suggested in the other chapters of this book to make and keep your relationship healthy.

By now you and your partner will have decided what you believe will help you achieve your goal. However, it is not enough to know what you are going to do and how. Reading and understanding are

just the first steps. It's like reading a book on how to ride a bicycle. Understanding the theory is good; however, you cannot say you know how to ride a bicycle until you actually go out and try riding. And just like riding a bicycle, whenever you are learning a new skill, expect that it will take some practice and that you will make mistakes.

The Power of Partnership

As you continue to work on your commitments there are a few helpful hints I want to share with you. The first is that most people find it easier to commit and follow through on something if they work together with another person. A loving partnership is an ideal situation.

The concept of working together may be illustrated with the following example:

Visualize yourself walking along the steel rail of a railway track. Your partner is walking along beside you on the other steel rail. As you walk along on your own, on top of this narrow steel rail, you may find it difficult to keep your balance. How far could you walk without losing your balance? Holding your hands out to the side will help you keep your balance. Perhaps you have done this on your own before and you have gone a great distance. What about your partner? How easy is it for your partner to keep their balance? Now imagine what it would be like if you walked alongside of your partner, and you joined hands. You both still held your other hand out to the side for balance, but between the two rails you held on to your partner's hand. You combine your strength and balance with your partner's as you walk along, side by side, hand in hand. How far could you go? Perhaps you could go as far as reaching your goal.

This example illustrates so beautifully that if you want to increase your chances of success, of meeting your goals and following through on your commitments, you should engage the help of another person. The motivating effect of a caring friend, a coach, a counselor, a group of supportive individuals sharing the same goals, just to name a few, are well documented. However, none of them can replace the powerful influence of a loving partner.

Working together as partners, you can encourage and support each other to meet and complete the goals you have set for yourselves.

With a little help from your partner, you increase your chances of sticking to your commitments by allowing your partner to support you, as well as to remind you whenever you fail to follow through. You might say that you are employing your partner as a loving reminder.

The basic approach is to give your partner a copy of your self-contract, and share what you plan to do to make your relationship better. By describing what goals you have set for yourself and how you plan to achieve them, your partner will be able to determine that you are meeting your goals. You then ask your partner to remind you of your goals whenever you fail to follow through on your commitment.

When I present this idea to my client couples, there are a few partners who are not too pleased. They protest, "It will just be another excuse for him to nag me about something else I failed to do," or "I don't want to give her another reason to tell me what to do." Obviously, I am not suggesting that you use this exercise as another excuse to beat up on each other. I realize that when you are not getting what you want, and what your partner has promised to give, you may be strongly tempted to lash out. Your reminder can take the form of a punishing statement: "You don't care enough about me or the relationship to even do a simple thing like…" You know the rest. What you should know about punishment is that while it may work to stop bad behaviors, it is incredibly inefficient when you want to encourage new, positive behaviors.

Our usual response when somebody disappoints us and fails to follow through on their promise, is to show our disapproval. Unfortunately, that kind of response seldom gets us what we want.

It usually leads to more disappointment. Therefore, if you really mean it when you say that you want to help, then follow through on your promise. You promised to remind your partner about the goal. So that's what you do. Kindly remind them, in a caring way.

If you really mean it when you say you want to help your partner, then the best thing you can do is to offer encouragement and recognition as they strive to achieve their goals. You can also help your partner celebrate when goals are reached. Remember how powerful recognition is? Well here is a good time to practice what you've learned. Recognition is reinforcing, and unlike punishment, it is a great way to motivate someone to continue good behavior. Remember some of the ways you have been reinforced, and how they worked? Think back. Perhaps, when you were young, you received a gold star for an assignment you worked hard to complete. Or a ribbon for a project you didn't think you had the skills to even begin. These rewards you received likely spurred you on to more hard work, and eventually the behavior itself, and the feeling of doing something well, was reward enough.

Now I realize you probably know all this stuff already. However, sometimes we need to be reminded of the powerful effect of positive reinforcement. We often get so caught up in our own disappointments that we forget that we ourselves have contributed to the result. Remember the effects of a "self-fulfilling prophecy?" Well, the same thing could happen here. When we say and believe that something is going to happen, it usually does because we make it happen. Words like "You never have listened to me, and you never will," can be quite prophetic. The fact is, when you have negative expectations you will also behave in a negative way. You then fail to use reinforcement, and begin to behave in a punishing manner.

If you really want to help each other to make your relationship better, then make the experience a pleasant one. Take every opportunity to compliment and recognize each other's efforts to make things better. Just one word of caution: Please do this only when it

comes from your heart. Your compliments and rewards should be genuine, not just another form of manipulation.

You are in this together, and you will reap the rewards together. Just like a "self-fulfilling prophecy," you will receive what you expect.

The Power of Your Thinking

"That's just the way I am. I can't change it." Have you ever made that statement? If you have, you are deceiving yourself. We all can change our behavior, at any time, at any age. You, too, can change and begin to do the things you choose to make a healthy relationship. The first step is to want to change. However, desire is not enough. You have to *believe* you can change.

Throughout history, there have been innumerable examples of ordinary people achieving the extraordinary. The one factor common to all of these successful people is that they believed they could do it. Now I realize that you are not reading this book to change the world, or to break any records. You just want to have a healthier relationship. You still need to be aware of how your own thinking will determine your success or failure. You need to apply the same principle as any other successful person.

Let's look at just one case of the incredible power of believing that you can achieve your goals:

It happened on May 6, 1954. That was the day Roger Bannister ran the mile in 3.594 minutes, and set a new world record. He became the first athlete in history to run a mile in less than four minutes—a record that medical and sport experts alike had said could *never* be broken. Many had tried to break this barrier previously, yet no one had ever done it. The experts suggested this barrier was real, and that human beings were not capable of running any faster. Then along came Roger who believed it could be done.

Roger Bannister, who was knighted in 1975, was a British physician who had a passion for running. He believed he could prove the experts were wrong. He trained very hard, and he kept practicing. Now you have to realize that for centuries other human beings had been doing this as well, yet they never broke the four-minute barrier. They settled for being the fastest person on earth, during that year. They believed they had run as fast as any human could, until that day in 1954 when Roger proved them wrong.

The incredible thing about Bannister's achievement was that it changed the belief systems of other runners. Less than two months later, the Australian athlete, John Landy, also broke the four-minute mile, and set another record of 3.58 minutes. Later that year Bannister defeated Landy in a mile race held in Vancouver, Canada. Even though neither set a new record, both Roger and John again broke the four-minute barrier. Today, you don't even qualify for a world-class event unless you run the mile in less than four minutes.

Sometimes we need another person to prove to us that something can be done. One person can help us to change our thinking, and thereby change our behavior. Why not look at the countless numbers of couples that have made their relationships better? You, too, can make it happen and have the relationship you desire. You can change yourself and be the kind of partner you want to be. As many couples have proven, your ability to create a healthy relationship depends greatly on your belief that you can. If you believe you can, you will. If you believe you can't, you won't.

Never underestimate the power of your own thinking.

I'm Just Not Motivated

The assumption that only some people are motivated is false. All of us are motivated. Some of us are just motivated to do nothing. And doing nothing can sometimes take a lot of work.

It is also misleading to assume that it takes an outside force to motivate us. The fact is that all motivation is self-motivation. Certainly, we can be influenced by someone else to take action. However, we need to be convinced about the benefit for ourselves, before we are willing to commit to an action or goal.

Similarly, we sometimes make an incorrect assumption about our partner's level of motivation. For example, if you see your partner working at a slow pace, you may assume he or she is lazy. However, your partner may be motivated by a desire to do a good job, and is simply taking more time in order to avoid mistakes. Slow or fast, it doesn't matter, as long as they do what they promised to do.

Another factor that may have been at the root of past, unhealthy behavior could be our expectation of what a good relationship "should" be. If our expectation is faulty, it may result in us trying to achieve something that is not realistic—for instance, trying to achieve some mythical, "perfect" relationship. Perfection is just not attainable by us mortals. If we continually try to achieve the impossible, we will just get frustrated, and eventually we will be motivated to give up.

The trick is to know what is realistic and what is not in your relationship, and to not give up until you have fulfilled your commitment. As Thomas Edison once said, "Many of life's failures are made by people who did not realize how close they were to success when they gave up." Working towards a better relationship is practical and within your reach. Don't give up.

Review your self-contract. Determine whether or not your promises are realistic, and be very honest with yourself as to what motivates you to follow through on your commitment.

Share your feelings with your partner and combine your powers of personal motivation to achieve your common goal for a healthy relationship.

Emotional Commitment

People make decisions with their head, and make commitments with their heart. There are all kinds of examples of how we do that. Think about a situation where you continue to deal with a certain store or sales person just because you *feel* good about going there. Or you keep buying the same type of car just because it *feels* right. You can't think of a rational reason why you do it, but you do it anyway.

The following is an actual example of this phenomenon:

During a brand loyalty test, people were asked which box of salt they would purchase. The tester had two boxes displayed. One was a box of brand name salt. The other box was a no-name brand. The potential buyers were told that the salt in the no-name box was the same as was in the brand name box. The testers made it clear that the no-name brand was actually produced and packaged by the same company as the familiar brand. It was also five cents cheaper. When asked which brand they would buy, the majority of consumers chose the familiar brand. When asked why they would pay five cents more for the same salt, the usual response was, "I've always bought that brand. It's what I grew up with."

This example shows how often we can be committed to something or someone, not for a rational reason but because it just feels right. Advertisers are very familiar with the power of emotional commitment and brand loyalty. That is why you will continue to see and hear commercial appeals that target our emotions.

If you truly want to make a commitment to yourself and your partner, it would be helpful for you to sit quietly and determine whether or not your promise "feels right" to you.

The most powerful commitment is one that makes sense in your head and feels right in your heart.

I Can See Myself Doing It

The power of visualization is another skill you can put to use. What this means is that you visualize yourself practicing your new behavior—for example, visualizing yourself having a successful resolution to a conflict with your partner.

One of the first books to make this concept popular was *Psycho-Cybernetics,* written by Dr. Maxwell Maltz. Dr. Maltz illustrates the power of our imagination in changing our behavior. The process involves you achieving a mental picture of yourself engaging in the desired activity. It is a technique that has definitely caught on in the sporting world. Many professional athletes now employ sport psychologists, who coach them in this technique to significantly improve their performance. Watch for this technique being demonstrated the next time you see downhill skiers prepare for a race. You will see them with eyes closed, imagining a successful run. Golf and tennis players have caught on to the same techniques and play the "inner game" before they step onto the fairway or court.

You may be interested in an experiment that was conducted to determine the impact of visualization on performance. This experiment involved two groups of young men with little experience in playing basketball. After measuring their performance (shooting hoops), one group was instructed to practice on the court. The other group was trained to visualize throwing the ball in the basket for half the practice time and then given the remaining time for actual practice.

The result showed that even though both groups spent the same amount of time learning this skill, the group that used the visualization techniques performed significantly better than the group that spent time solely on physical practice.

Couples have used visualization to build confidence and self-esteem, and to create more positive behavioral patterns. The process involves using positive mental images and practicing seeing yourself as successful and confident. You can use this technique for con-

flict resolution, improving your communication skills, reducing the power of the "hot buttons" in a conflict, slowing down your anger response, and learning relaxation techniques, to name just a few examples. I would suggest you use visualization to assist the learning process of the behaviors you have listed on your self-contract.

The process of visualization is actually very simple. It works in the same manner as rehearsing for a play, only in this case you are rehearsing for real-life scenarios. Form a picture in your mind of the person you want to be or the behavior you want to acquire. Practice seeing yourself in the role you have chosen until you are very familiar with it. Like the thinking or cognitive approach, which requires you to *believe in your ability to do it*, the visual approach requires you to *see yourself doing it* successfully. As you practice the new behavior in your mind's eye, what happens is that you learn more quickly than simply practicing in real life. This is just like the results achieved by professional athletes.

What is most powerful is if you use a combination of these visualization techniques and practice them together with your loving partner.

It Takes Practice, Practice, Practice

You have seen the word "practice" used numerous times in this book. I have done that because it is a very important piece of the puzzle. I remind you that you cannot say you truly know how to do something unless you have practiced and been able to successfully do it consistently over a prolonged period of time.

The other piece of the puzzle is that you need to keep doing it until it becomes a habit. One of the first persons to suggest this was Aristotle, who said, "We are what we repeatedly do. Excellence, then, is not an act, but a habit."

More recently, Stephen Covey, in his incredibly popular book *The 7 Habits of Highly Effective People,* states, "Habits can be learned and unlearned. But I also know it isn't a quick fix. It involves a process and a tremendous commitment."

The power of a habit is a very important concept to understand. Remember my original question, "Why are some promises easier to keep than others?" Well, knowing what to do, and having a strong desire to do it, is part of the solution to keeping your promises. The other part is doing the behavior so often so that you would actually miss it if you *didn't* do it.

Think about some behaviors you engage in that you would find difficult to change. Perhaps you remember a promise you made on New Year's Eve that you forgot about a short time later. What was missing from the equation? It could be that you hadn't really committed yourself to it. However, it could very well be that you gave up too soon. It had not become part of your routine. Having the desire to do something is good, but sometimes we find it hard to motivate ourselves to do something that we find difficult. Knowing *what* to do helps as well, but until it becomes easy and pleasant to do we can find ourselves making excuses to avoid it.

The final "C" then is to keep working on the other six "C"s until they become a habit!

Keeping Your Promise

One of the best ways to increase your chances of keeping your commitments and meeting your goals is to **write out a self-contract**. Making a contract with yourself may not stop you from breaking your promises, but it is an effective way of building your commitment to follow through on them.

This is the last step in the 7 "C's" for a healthy relationship. You

have determined what you want to do for your relationship, now all that remains is for you to follow through on your promises. By the way, this kind of advice goes back as far as the first century B.C., when the Greek philosopher Epictetus said, "First say to yourself what you would be, and then do what you have to do." I suppose that even back then people had problems keeping their commitments.

It is now time to review *your* commitments. Go back to each of the six previous sections and decide if there are any other promises that you want to add to your self-contract. Finish transferring these promises you have made to your self-contract. There are two copies on the following pages.

You can also order additional, 8 1/2 by 11" full-color copies by logging on to our Web site: **www.thecouplescoach.com**

Once you have written down your promises, review them with your loving partner, renew your commitment to doing them, and sign and date your contract. Keep your contract in a safe place and refer to it occasionally as a reminder of your promises.

Vitamin C for Couples

Seven "C"s For a Healthy Relationship

Self Contract

Caring

I will ______________________________

Change

I will ______________________________

Communication

I will ______________________________

Connection

I will ______________________________

Conflict

I will ______________________________

Creativity

I will ______________________________

Commitment

I will ______________________________

Signed by: ______________________________

Date: ____________________

Luke De Sadeleer
www.thecouplescoach.com

Email: luke@thecouplescoach.com Tel: (613) 762-5210 Fax: (613) 727-4829

Vitamin C for Couples
Seven "C"s For a Healthy Relationship

Self Contract

Caring
I will ______________________________

Change
I will ______________________________

Communication
I will ______________________________

Connection
I will ______________________________

Conflict
I will ______________________________

Creativity
I will ______________________________

Commitment
I will ______________________________

Signed by: ______________________________
Date: ________________

Luke De Sadeleer
www.thecouplescoach.com

Email: luke@thecouplescoach.com Tel: (613) 762-5210 Fax: (613) 727-4829

My Wish for You

Sometimes the best teachings come from a children's book. Whenever I think about what it means to be "really" loved, I am always reminded of that wonderful book written by Margery Williams, called *The Velveteen Rabbit.* The story describes a stuffed rabbit who wants to learn how to become real. The rabbit is told by a wise old toy called the Skin Horse, that it actually only happens under certain conditions:

"It doesn't happen all at once," said the Skin Horse. "You become. It takes a long time. That's why it doesn't often happen to people who break easily, or have sharp edges, or who have to be carefully kept. Generally, by the time you are Real, most of your hair has been loved off, and your eyes drop out and you get loose in the joints and very shabby. But these things don't matter at all, because once you are Real you can't be ugly, except to people who don't understand."

My sincere wish for you, the loving couples who have read this book, is that you give enough love and get enough love so that you become "Real."

Keep in Touch

My dear loving partners, I am firmly convinced that if you practice the seven "C"s illustrated in *Vitamin C for Couples*, you will have a healthy relationship that will withstand any challenge. In fact, I'd welcome your success stories. Let me know how my book has influenced you. I appreciate your sharing your experience, even though I may not be able to respond to each of you personally.

May you live a long and healthy life together.

You can contact me by e-mail at luke@thecouplescoach.com, by fax at (613) 727-4829, or send comments to Luke De Sadeleer c/o Creative Bound Inc., Box 424, Carp, Ontario, Canada K0A 1L0.

For information about presentations, workshops, special events and products, log on to my Web site: **www.thecouplescoach.com**

Bibliography and Suggested Reading

Adler, Ronald. Rosenfeld, Lawrence.; Towne, Neil: *Interplay: The Process of Interpersonal Communication,* 4th ed. New York: Holt, Rinehart and Winston, Inc. 1989.

Augsburger, David. *The Freedom of Forgiveness.* Chicago, IL: Moody Press, 1973.

Bach, George and Peter Wyden. *The Intimate Enemy: How to Fight Fair in Love and Marriage.* New York: Avon Books, 1970.

Bandler, Richard and John Grinder. *Frogs into Princes: Neuro-Linguistic Programming.* Moab, UT: Real People Press, 1979.

Barbach, Lonnie Garfield. *For Yourself: The Fulfillment of Female Sexuality.* New York: Doubleday & Company, 1975.

Beck, Aaron T. *Cognitive Therapy and the Emotional Disorders.* New York: International Universities Press, 1976.

Beck, Aaron T. *Love Is Never Enough: How Couples Can Overcome Misunderstandings, Resolve Conflicts, and Solve Relationship Problems Through Cognitive Therapy.* New York: Harper & Row, 1988.

Berne, Eric. *Games People Play.* New York: Grove Press, 1964.

Bowlby, John. *Attachment and Loss: Vol. 1. Attachment.* New York: Basic Books, 1969.

Bowlby, John. *A Secure Base.* New York: Basic Books, 1988.

Buscaglia, Leo. *Loving Each Other.* New York: Holt, Rinehart and Winston, 1984.

Cameron, Julia. *The Artist's Way: A Spiritual Path to Higher Creativity.* New York: Jeremy P. Tarcher/Putnam, 1992.

Carlson, Richard and Joseph Bailey. *Slowing Down to the Speed of Life: How to Create a More Peaceful, Simpler Life from the Inside Out.* New York: HarperCollins Publishers, Inc., 1998.

Charlesworth, Edward A, and Ronald G. Nathan. *Stress Management: A Comprehensive Guide to Wellness.* New York: McClelland and Stewart Ltd., 1984.

Clifton, Donald and Paula Nelson. *Soar With Your Strengths.* New York: Delacorte Press, 1992.

Covey, Stephen. *The 7 Habits of Highly Effective People.* New York: Simon & Schuster, 1990.

Creighton, James L. *How Loving Couples Fight.* Fairfield, Connecticut: Aslan Publishing, 1998.

Ellis, Albert and Robert Harper. *A New Guide To Rational Living.* Englewood Cliffs, NJ: Prentice-Hall, 1975.

Ellis, Albert and Russell Grieger. *RET: Handbook of Rational Emotive Therapy.* New York: Springer Publishing Company, 1977.

Fromme, Allan. *The Ability to Love.* North Hollywood, CA: Wilshire Book Company, 1965.

Flaherty, James. *Coaching: Evoking Excellence in Others.* Boston, MS: Butterworth-Heinemann, 1999.

Fulghum, Robert. *All I Really Need to Know I Learned in Kindergarten.* Toronto, ON: Random House of Canada Ltd., 1989.

Gaylin, Willard. *Feelings.* New York: Ballantine Books, 1980.

Gaylin, Willard. *Rediscovering Love.* New York: Viking Penguin Inc., 1986.

Goleman, Daniel. *Emotional Intelligence.* New York: Bantam Books, 1995.

Gottman, John and Nan Silver. *The Seven Principles for Making Marriage Work.* New York: Crown Publishers Inc., 1999.

Gottman, John. *Why Marriages Succeed or Fail: How You Can Make Yours Last.* New York: Fireside, 1995.

Gottman, John. *What Predicts Divorce?* Hillsdale, NJ: Lawrence Erlbaum Associates, Inc., 1993.

Greenberger, Dennis and Christine A. Padesky. *Mind Over Mood: A Cognitive Therapy Treatment Manual for Clients.* New York: The Guilford Press, 1995.

Irvine, David. *Simple Living in a Complex World.* Calgary, AB: RedStone Publishing, 1997.

Jampolsky, Gerald G. *Forgiveness: The Greatest Healer of All.* Hillsboro, Oregon: Beyond Words Publishing, Inc., 1999.

Jampolsky, Gerald G. *Love Is Letting Go of Fear.* Berkeley, CA: Celestial Arts, 1979.

Johnson, Susan M. *Creating Connection: The Practice of Emotionally Focused Marital Therapy.* New York: Brunner/Mazel, Inc., 1996.

Jong, Erica. *How to Save Your Own Life.* New York: Holt, Rinehart and Winston, 1977.

Keirsey, David, and Bates, Marilyn. *Please Understand Me.* Del Mar, CA: Prometheus Nemesis, 1978.

Lair, Jess. *I Ain't Much, Baby—But I'm All I've Got.* Greenwich, CT: Fawcett Publications, Inc., 1972.

Lankton, Stephen R. *Practical Magic: The Clinical Applications of Neuro-Linguistic Programming.* Cupertino, CA: Meta Publications, 1979.

Lessor, Richard. *Love & Marriage and Trading Stamps.* IL: Argus Communications, 1971.

Lewis, David. *In and Out of Love: The Mystery of Personal Attraction.* London: Metheun, 1985.

Lewis, Thomas, Fari Amini, Richard Lannon. *A General Theory of Love.* New York: Random House, 2000.

Maltz, Maxwell. *Psycho-Cybernetics.* Englewood Cliffs, NJ: Prentice-Hall, Inc., 1973.

McRae, Brad. *Negotiating and Influencing Skills: The Art of Creating and Claiming Value.* Thousand Oaks, CA: Sage Publications, Inc., 1998.

Mehrabian, Albert. *Nonverbal Communication.* Chicago, IL: Aldine-Atherton, 1972.

Meichenbaum, Donald H. *Cognitive Behavior Modification.* New York: Plenum, 1977.

Myers, Isabel Briggs, with Myers, Peter. *Gifts Differing.* Palo Alto, CA: Consulting Psychologists Press, 1993.

O'Donohue, John. *Eternal Echoes: Exploring Our Yearning to Belong.* New York: HarperCollins Publishers, Inc., 1999.

Ornish, Dean. *Love & Survival: The Scientific Basis for the Healing Power of Intimacy.* New York: HarperCollins, 1998.

Powell, John. *Why Am I Afraid to Love?* Niles, IL: Argus Communications Co., 1972.

Prather, Hugh. *Notes to Myself: My struggle to become a person.* Toronto, ON: Bantam Books, 1976.

Rogers, Carl. *Becoming Partners: Marriage and Its Alternatives.* New York: Delacorte Press, 1973.

Satir, Virginia. *Peoplemaking.* Palo Alto, CA: Science and Behavior Books, Inc., 1976.

Selye, Hans. *Stress Without Distress.* New York: Lippincott, 1980.

Smith, Adam. *Powers Of Mind.* New York: Ballantine Books, 1976.

Spitz, Rene. "Hospitalism: an inquiry into the genesis of psychiatric conditions in early childhood." *Psychoanalytic Study of the Child,* 1945.

Stevens, Barry. *Don't Push the River: It Flows by Itself.* Berkeley, CA: Celestial Arts, 1985.

Stewart, John. *Bridges, Not Walls,* 4th ed. New York: Random House, 1986.

Urichuck, Bob. *Online for Life: The 12 Disciplines for Living Your Dreams.* Carp, ON: Creative Bound Inc., 2000.

Walsh, Anthony. *The Science of Love: Understanding Love and Its Effects on Mind and Body.* Buffalo, NY: Prometheus Books, 1991

Watson, David and Roland Tharp. *Self-Directed Behavior,* 3rd ed. Monterey, CA: Brooks/Cole Publishing Company, 1981

West-Meads, Zelda. *The Trouble With You.* London: Hodder & Stoughton, 1996.

Wile, Daniel. *After the Fight: Using Your Disagreements to Build a Stronger Relationship.* New York: The Guilford Press, 1993.

Wile, Daniel. *After the Honeymoon: How Conflict Can Improve Your Relationship.* New York: Wiley, 1988.

Williams, Margery. *The Velveteen Rabbit.* New York: Henry Holt, 1983.

Young, Howard. *A Rational Counseling Primer.* New York: The Institute for Rational Living Inc., 1974.

Zunin, Leonard and Natalie Zunin. *Contact: The First Four Minutes.* New York: Ballantine Books, Inc., 1973.

Books that inspire, help and heal

We hope you have enjoyed
Vitamin C for Couples
Seven "C"s for a Healthy Relationship

To order additional copies of *Vitamin C for Couples* by Luke De Sadeleer, please contact Creative Bound Inc. at 1-800-287-8610 (toll-free, North America) or (613) 831-3641. Associations, institutions, businesses and retailers—ask about our wholesale discounts for bulk orders.

ISBN 0-921165-68-4 $18.95 CAN
$15.95 US

Do you know who you are?
Do you love what you're doing?
Do you have what you want out of life?
Do you *know* what you want out of life?
Are you "committed" to anything?
Are you thankful for each new day?

If you answered "no" to any of these questions, but want to say YES! to all of them, this book will inspire you to take control of your life. Bob Urichuck's acclaimed 12 Disciplines will provide you with a step-by-step, *inside-out* approach to finding the authentic you. With discipline, direction, and new tools in hand, you'll soon be living the life of your dreams!

Internationally respected speaker and trainer Bob Urichuck helps individuals and organizations identify their objectives and the disciplines needed to achieve them. The results are measurable and lasting.

Online for Life: *the 12 Disciplines for Living Your Dreams*

ISBN 0-921165-65-X $19.95 CAN
200 pages $15.95 US

***Call to order*: 1-800-287-8610** *(toll-free in North America)*
***or write to*: Creative Bound Inc.**
Box 424, Carp, Ontario, Canada K0A 1L0

www.creativebound.com